MANDATORY MOTHERHOOD

MANDATORY MOTHERHOOD

THE TRUE MEANING OF
"RIGHT TO LIFE"

GARRETT HARDIN

BEACON PRESS *BOSTON*

"One Hundred and Twenty Children Born After Application for Therapeutic Abortion Refused," by Hans Forssman and Inga Thuwe, reprinted by permission from *Acta Psychiatrica Scandinavica* 42 © 1966.

Copyright © 1974 by Garrett Hardin

Beacon Press books are published under the auspices of the Unitarian Universalist Association

Simultaneous publication in Canada by Saunders of Toronto, Ltd.

Published in simultaneous hardcover and paperback editions

All rights reserved

Printed in the United States of America

9 8 7 6 5 4 3 2 1

Library of Congress Cataloging in Publication Data

Hardin, Garrett James, 1915–
  Mandatory motherhood.
  1. Abortion—United States.   I. Title.
[DNLM: 1. Abortion, Induced. HQ767.5.U5 H262m]
HQ767.5.U5H36   301   74–4880
ISBN 0–8070–2176–8
ISBN 0–8070–2177–6 (pbk.)

With Thanks to—

HYLA
PETER
SHARON
DAVID

*For Making Parenthood
a Strenuous but Eminently
Worthwhile Experience*

ACKNOWLEDGMENTS

Though I am not much of a believer in group creativity, I am keenly aware of how many of the ideas in this book are the product of the interaction between myself and others. Since the time I gave my first speech on abortion in 1963 I have been led to insight after insight by my auditors. It should be no surprise that most of these have been women. To a large extent I have become an instrument through which the other subculture speaks. I am grateful for the privilege.

I have never known the names of most of the people who have helped me; and such is the fragility of memory that I can now recall only the latest of my benefactors. But let me at least thank these.

First of all comes Jane, my wife, who has acted as eyes and ears for me in coming to know the subculture I cannot belong to. In criticizing this latest version of my argument, Ruth Roemer, Kathy Maurer, Florence Hardin, Donald Lesh, Carl Stover, and Rodney Shaw have been most helpful. Harriet Pilpel has contributed not only useful criticisms but also valuable advice in practical matters. I am grateful to Hans Forssman and Inga Thuwe (and to the publishers of *Acta Psychiatrica Scandinavica*) for kind permission to republish their classic study.

The title of the book is the product of a brainstorming session with family and friends, which began with my earlier coinage "compulsory pregnancy"; the culminating change in the series of terms was rung by Tom Cory, to whom I am especially grateful.

CONTENTS

1. Right to Life Equals Mandatory Motherhood — 1
2. Ruling Out Religion — 6
3. Abortion Prohibition, an Imprudent Experiment — 9
4. Close, Naked, Natural — 14
5. The Indispensable Backstop — 17
6. Margaret's Story — 21
7. Pregnancy as Punishment — 24
8. The Two Subcultures — 28
9. The Community's Interest — 34
10. The Sixth Commandment — 40
11. The Thin Edge of the Wedge — 43
12. When Does Life Begin? — 46
13. Truth's Day in Court — 50
14. Who Is Responsible? And for What? — 55
15. How Valuable Is Information? — 59
16. You've Murdered Beethoven! — 63
17. The Earlier the Better — 66
18. Cruel Logic — 69
19. The Ultimate Right? — 72
20. You Can't Photograph Morality — 74
21. What Is Informed Consent? — 79
22. Premature Simplification — 81

23.	How a Minority Can Take Over	86
24.	A Cascade of Consequences	90
25.	Prospects for a Sane Society	94

Appendixes

A.	Organizations Supporting Abortion	101
B.	Gallup Poll on Abortion	103
C.	The Swedish Study	105
D.	Reading List	133
E.	Educational and Activist Organizations	135

1
RIGHT TO LIFE EQUALS MANDATORY MOTHERHOOD

Mandatory motherhood? Surely this isn't serious!

But it is. Dead serious: a small but energetic minority is dedicated to forcing motherhood onto women who don't want to be mothers. These passionate people wouldn't dream of trying to bring back compulsory servitude (i.e., slavery). But, strangely, they see no inconsistency in trying to institute mandatory motherhood for women whose birth-control methods have failed them.

The passionate minority just may succeed.

How did we get into this mess? The story can be briefly told. Until about 1870 abortion was legal in the United States (though not advisable in those days of primitive medicine). Then, in rapid succession, one state after another passed laws against abortion. Some forbade it completely. Others permitted it only to save the life of the mother. Six states permitted abortion "to save the life of the child," though how that was possible the legislators never told us. That so incredible a law could be passed strongly suggests that many legislators were simply unwilling to think about abortion. They just passed laws with their minds closed, and moved on to other matters. Their ill-considered laws were not subjected to further legislative review for almost a century.

Restrictive laws made it difficult, dangerous, and expensive for women to avoid unwanted motherhood during that century. There was irony and tragedy in the situation: the abortion-prohibition laws were all unconstitutional. A few keen lawyers said as much toward the end, but they could not prove they were right. That takes a test case—and where were they to get one? Justice is slower than procreation. A woman who is pregnant against her will can't wait for the Supreme Court to make up its mind. She goes out and finds an illegal abortionist. It's faster. And cheaper.

Despite the difficulties, test cases were finally brought to the Supreme Court, and the justices spoke on January 22, 1973. The main points of the Supreme Court decision can be quickly summarized. By a striking 7 to 2 majority the Court threw out *all* the state prohibition laws, declaring that American women have a Constitutional right to free themselves from unwanted pregnancy. States cannot infringe on that right in the first three months, but may make minor restrictions later.

Those of us who had worked for the repeal of abortion laws were ecstatic: we thought our work was finished. How wrong we were! Within a few weeks, already existing Right-to-Life groups stepped up their antiabortion activities. Some two hundred restrictive bills were introduced into the legislatures of more than forty states. The number of antiabortion letters to the editor in newspapers increased markedly. Spokesmen for Right-to-Life got bookings with service clubs throughout the country. On the first anniversary of the Supreme Court decision 6000 peaceful Right-to-Lifers staged a demonstration on Capitol Hill in Washington, and "mourning boxes" (like the one reproduced from the *Santa Barbara News-Press*, 22 January 1974) appeared in newspapers throughout the country.

> **IN MEMORY**
>
> of
>
> 1.6 million babies who have been killed
>
> under the Supreme Court Decree
>
> of January 22, 1973
>
> If you are interested in saving unborn babies' lives write to: Right to Life League of Southern California Santa Barbara Chapter 609 East Haley St. Santa Barbara 93103

Several Constitutional amendments were in committee by this time. Would they eventually be passed and ratified? Or would they die somewhere along the line? No one could say, but pass or fail, it was obvious that the need for public education was greater than ever.

If an antiabortion bill passed in the present session of Congress, it would be necessary to inform the public about the true issues so it could knowledgeably instruct state legislators how to vote on ratification. If all antiabortion bills were defeated in the present session of

Congress, new ones would undoubtedly be offered in the next session.

And the next . . . and the next.

It was a case of "future shock"—change coming faster than much of the public was prepared for. The Supreme Court took a giant step while many citizens were still fumbling with their shoelaces. There's no relief from future shock without more information—hence, this book.

The Constitutional amendments offered by Right-to-Lifers vary, but one will serve as a typical example. In 1973 Representative Lawrence Hogan of Maryland offered the following bill:

> Neither the United States, nor any State shall deprive any human being, from the moment of conception, of life without due process of law; nor deny to any human being, from the moment of conception . . . the equal protection of the law.

If such an amendment should become the law, how would it change our lives? In countless ways, all following from the radical act of defining all stages of development, "from the moment of conception," as human beings in the full meaning of the law. The ultimate results of such a law are revealed in the following logical sequence.

1. There is no due process of law whereby one human being, or the state, can deprive another *and innocent* human being of life. (Capital punishment is only for the guilty.)

2. A Right-to-Life Amendment asserts that all em-

bryonic stages, from the fertilized egg onward, are human beings *period*.

3. An embryo is certainly "innocent" of all wrongdoing.

4. Therefore, an embryo cannot be deliberately aborted and killed.

5. Therefore, a woman who found herself unwillingly pregnant would be compelled by law to become a mother.

That is mandatory motherhood.

A Right-to-Life Amendment is a Mandatory Motherhood Amendment.

Unfair! You've renamed the amendment so as to bring emotions into the picture.

Not for the first time. *Different* emotions. The original name also played on the emotions. So let's be fair and give the total consequences, both immediate and ultimate, in the name of the amendment proposed:

The Right - to - Life - of - Even - the - Tiniest - Embryo - Even - Though - This - Inevitably - Produces - Mandatory-Motherhood Amendment.

That's fair (but unmanageable).

What all this illustrates, of course, is that in choosing names for proposed laws proponents don't try to be fair. They try to win.

We cannot blame them. But we, the people on whom laws are perpetrated, must protect ourselves by suspecting every name. We must look for other, equally accurate, ways of naming each bill so as to uncover its unmentioned consequences. Whenever someone speaks of the Right-to-Life Amendment we should immediately respond by saying:

"Oh, yes—you mean the Mandatory Motherhood Amendment."

2
RULING OUT RELIGION

The conflict over abortion is always in danger of becoming prolonged along religious lines: Catholics versus Protestants. A list (compiled in 1972) of organizations publicly supporting modification or repeal of the abortion-prohibition laws showed not a single Catholic organization among the total of sixty-three, though Baptists, Jews, Episcopalians, Moravians, Presbyterians, Methodists, Unitarians, and Quakers were included. (See Appendix A for the list.) Later, the organization Catholics for a Free Choice joined the group, not so much supporting abortion as opposing the Right-to-Life position of making the issue a legal one.

We can ill afford a conflict polarized along religious lines. Fortunately Right-to-Lifers insist that the conflict is deeper than sectarianism—and all of us should endorse this position.

It is true that chapters of the Right to Life League have always been started within the circle of power of a parish church, and initially peopled almost entirely by Roman Catholics. But many non-Catholics hold the same view, and chapters have been alert to move these people into official positions so they can speak for the group.

Indubitable truth: *not all Right-to-Lifers are Catholics.*

On the other hand it is also indubitably true that not all Catholics are Right-to-Lifers or even agree with the Lifers' position. The only Catholic member of the Supreme Court, Justice William J. Brennan, Jr., voted with the majority. A small minority of priests even support freely elective abortion.

Despite a great difference between organizations supporting or opposing voluntary abortion, a Gallup Poll showed no appreciable difference between individuals of the two main religious groupings. In June 1972 pollsters asked this question: "Do you agree that the decision to have an abortion should be made solely by a woman and her physician?" Of the Protestants, 65 percent answered yes; of the Catholics, 56 percent. The difference is no doubt statistically significant, but not politically so. Note that a majority of both groups favored elective abortion. (There was also little difference between Republicans and Democrats; and between men and women. The full results are given in Appendix B.)

If history is any guide, it looks as if the progress of Catholic opinion on abortion is repeating the earlier progression of thought on contraception. I am talking about the opinion of parishioners, of course. The clergy is somewhat restrained by the organization, and the Vatican seems to be frozen in position. But the rest of the living organism of the church moves, and outsiders should be chary of criticizing it for moving too slowly.

The Church *does* move.

In the meantime, the Right-to-Lifers—who include both Catholics and Protestants—are marshaling their forces to undo the abortion decisions of the Supreme Court. Three routes are open to them.

First: *statutory harassment.*

On the domestic scene hundreds of bills introduced into state legislatures and the Congress are designed to hog-tie abortion procedures. For example, some bills forbid using welfare funds to pay for abortion. This would create one kind of medicine for the poor, another for the rich. All such discriminatory measures will undoubtedly be thrown out by the courts on constitutional grounds.

But during the time between legislative passage and judicial repudiation, such laws can be effective in many communities. Hospital administrators are not noted for their courage. District attorneys must get themselves reelected. Doctors don't want trouble. And so, a patently unconstitutional mandatory motherhood law can be operative in some communities until the courts throw it out.

On the foreign scene, statutory harassment may be even more effective. Riders have been attached to foreign-aid bills canceling all grants if any money is used for abortion. Mandatory motherhood again, this time abroad. It is unlikely that much of a political force can be organized in the United States to oppose injustice abroad, so such laws (if passed) will probably stand.

Second: *Constitutional amendment by minority maneuvers.*

It takes a two-thirds majority in both houses of Congress to pass a Constitutional amendment, and two-thirds of the states must ratify it before it can become law. Since approximately two-thirds of the electorate are against mandatory motherhood it might seem impossible to push a prohibition amendment through.

But it isn't. There are mechanisms by which a representative democracy can (paradoxically) act undemocratically. These will be discussed later.

Third: *Constitutional amendment by persuasion.*

The Right-to-Lifers would like to build a majority base supporting abortion-prohibition. Tirelessly, they lecture to civic groups, seeking to reverse the trend toward elective abortion. It is the right of every individual and group in a democracy to attempt to persuade others. If the Right-to-Lifers overturn the Supreme Court decisions and, by thoroughly democratic means, reestablish the prohibition of abortion we should suspect that either their case is better or their opponents are lazier (or both).

3
ABORTION PROHIBITION, AN IMPRUDENT EXPERIMENT

Suppose the Right-to-Lifers turn public opinion around and persuade, say, 75 percent of the populace that we should have an abortion-prohibition amendment. Suppose the amendment were passed and ratified. Would that be the end of the matter? After all, it's "majority rule" in a democracy. Isn't a majority all we need for stable law?

Is there anyone so naïve as to believe *that?* Have we so soon forgotten Prohibition?

The Volstead Act—the alcohol-prohibition amendment—was passed in 1919 and became effective in 1920. There was no Gallup Poll then, but probably the majority was in favor of the amendment. It took another Constitutional Amendment to repeal the Volstead Act thirteen years later. Thirteen years of a "noble experiment," as President Hoover called it. What legacy did it leave?

Truths in history are not as certain as the "laws" of science, but it is generally agreed that the principal legacies of Prohibition were two:

1. Organized crime
2. A widespread contempt of the law among non-criminal elements of society

Some of the criminal organization is still with us more than forty years later. And widespread disrespect of the law persists.

The price of noble experiments is high.

Alcohol prohibition didn't work. Shall we now embark on abortion prohibition? It could be argued that this would not be so dangerous an experiment as alcohol prohibition, because abortions have been legal for only a short time; whereas alcohol, at the time Prohibition came in, had been legal since time immemorial.

A plausible argument.

But it fails to take account of the fantastic changes that have taken place in the last decade.

The abortion-reform movement began about 1960 in the United States. In 1967 two states passed the first reform laws. And in 1973 the Supreme Court outlawed abortion prohibition. If an abortion-prohibition Amendment were passed now, would this merely end a brief interlude, setting the clock back to where it was in 1960?

No: the clock of history can never be set back. We

"accepted" (so to speak) the prohibition of abortion before; but it is doubtful if we ever will again. The way we used to accept the law was by secretly violating it. It was estimated that about a million abortions were illegally performed every year, around 1960. The reason so massive a violation of the law did not lead to reform action was because of the personal, secret nature of the act.

Those who violated the Volstead Act did so together, in good fellowship. They stimulated one another to take political action. By contrast, abortion prohibition was violated in a lonely, nonsocial way. Victorian taboos interfered with public action.

Now all this is changed. Since 1960 the following significant changes have taken place:

1. The word *abortion* is no longer censored. (As of 1960 the stylebooks of many newspapers did not allow the word to be printed. "Illegal operation" was the commonest euphemism.)

2. The word *abortion* is no longer tabooed. (Most "nice" people—even women who had had abortions—couldn't bring themselves to speak the word in the old days.)

3. The women's movement has greatly altered women's attitudes toward repressive laws and practices.

4. The concern for social justice is much greater now. (Under the old illegal system poor women could not get safe abortions. Many impoverished women aborted themselves, and some of them died. Such discrimination on the basis of income is no longer regarded as tolerable.)

5. Doctors are no longer ashamed to perform abor-

tions. (Thousands of physicians now appreciate the woman's point of view. It is unrealistic to suppose that they will all passively accept a new prohibition law.)

6. Women now know that abortion is not as dangerous as its alternative, childbirth. (At the last reading, an early abortion was only one-eighth as dangerous as a normal childbirth. The risk continues to be lowered by further improvements in abortion technique. Requiring a woman to complete her pregnancy is requiring her to take a greater risk rather than a lesser.)

7. People now know that early abortions can be performed by competent personnel in very simple (but clean) surroundings. (No need for fancy hospitals. It is easy to hide illegal setups that are quite adequate.)

Legal or illegal, it is doubtful if abortion will ever again be as dangerous as it once was. For many years the Los Angeles county hospital, for example, had one ward devoted entirely to septic abortion cases. These were women who had been aborted by rank amateurs (sometimes themselves), and had ended up with massive infections. The ward had 90 beds, and it was always full.

Three years after a permissive California law was passed, this ward was phased out of existence. Once women could get legal abortions from proper doctors they stopped resorting to illegal, incompetent ones.

If abortion prohibition is reestablished the septic rate will probably never again go as high as it once was. Better methods of abortion have since been developed. (Note: these improvements in medicine were made in places where abortion was legal. An illegal system seldom produces medical advances.) Knowledge of the new methods is now widespread, and could survive recriminalization. The infection and death rates from illegal abortions would probably be less than they used to be.

The clock of history can never be turned back to exactly where it was before. A new abortion-prohibition law would surely be flouted on a far larger scale. The operation is no longer considered shameful; and women are less likely than ever to submit to mandatory motherhood.

Police would be required to enforce abortion prohibition. What would the consequences be?

Al Capone the Second?

A new Mafia?

At the very least, a new disrespect for the law. Can society afford more disrespect?

Philosophers of ethics distinguish between morality and prudence. Prudence is regarded as a sort of lower level of morality, but it is sometimes more important than pure morality because imprudent behavior often leads to a decay of morality generally.

Even if Right-to-Lifers are correct in their ethical judgment that abortion should be prohibited, they are most imprudent if they settle for a mere three-quarters majority in restricting the freedom of others.

If they are prudent, Right-to-Lifers will not push for an abortion-prohibition law until they have a great majority. But that's asking for an almost inhuman kind of self-restraint.

Our experience with alcohol prohibition showed that a mere majority is not enough in restricting some sorts of human behavior. How much is enough? 85 percent? 90 percent? 95 percent? No one knows.

But it is tragic when legal prohibition is instituted prematurely.

4
CLOSE, NAKED, NATURAL

Whatever their eventual political success, Right-to-Lifers have already performed a real educational service: they have forced more people to think about deep scientific and ethical questions. Questions like:

What is life?
What is the value of life?
Are all lives equally valuable?

Though they have made people think deeply, I don't think Right-to-Lifers have helped them to think well. As a biologist I know that the word *life* does not stand for a simple concept: it's easy to arrive at foolish conclusions if one has no more knowledge about life than Aristotle had more than two thousand years ago. (How would our airplanes fly if we had not mastered any physics later than Aristotle?)

A lot has been learned about the nature and value of life in the last century, particularly in the last forty years. This new knowledge is eminently relevant to the questions Right-to-Lifers raise. But, apparently, almost none of it is known to them.

It is often asserted that science and ethics are two completely separate, sovereign worlds of the intellect. Ethicists favor this view; most scientists do not. The closer one looks at the methods of science the more deeply one is impressed with the fact that even in the choice of methods ethics is involved.

One of the oldest scientific societies in the world is the Royal Society of London. It publishes several journals in which scientists describe new theories and findings. When the Society was started more than three centuries ago the founders decided (as Thomas Sprat tells us) that in their communications with others the members should try to return "to the primitive purity and shortness" of speech when men "delivered themselves of so many ideas in an almost equal number of words." The Society, said Sprat, exacted from its members "a close, naked, natural way of speaking; positive expressions; clear senses . . . preferring the language of artisans, countrymen, and merchants, before that of wits and scholars."

"A close, naked, natural way of speaking"—this, the proper preference of scientists, amounts to an ethical choice.

The policy described by Sprat is not without its contradictions. For instance, Sprat recommends that the language used should satisfy two criteria:

(a) it should be "close, naked, natural," and

(b) it should be the language of ordinary people ("artisans, countrymen, and merchants").

Unfortunately, in controversial matters, the language of ordinary people is often *not* naked. All too often it is clothed in emotional allusions that have accumulated over the centuries. Unacknowledged emotion interferes with precise analysis.

Contrast, for example, the two words *womb* and *uterus*. Anatomically, they are exact synonyms. But not emotionally. *Womb,* the word of artisans and merchants—and poets—carries a rich freight of emotional connotations that interfere with rational discussion. *Uterus* is a much less familiar word to nonbiologists, but for that reason it is virtually naked of connotations. It will be preferred here.

In analyzing controversial ideas we should always choose naked words over those wrapped in connotations. If we don't, we may unwittingly derive conclusions from the connotations rather than from the core meanings of words.

What shall we call that which is not yet born, but which will be called a *child* after birth? There are three possibilities:

> a fetus
> an embryo
> an unborn child.

Technical distinctions are sometimes made between the first two, but these distinctions are irrelevant to our problems here so we will use the words *fetus* and *embryo* indifferently. The second will be used most of the time.

What about the term *unborn child*? This term will never be used in this book, save in italics or between quotation marks.

Why not?

How often do you see references to an *unborn voter*? Or an *unborn senior citizen*?

Attaching the adjective *unborn* to the name of a stage that will be reached only after birth is a sneaky way of implying that the powers, privileges, and rights of a later stage belong also to an earlier one. It is a sneaky way of bringing in a premature, and unexamined, conclusion.

The question we want to examine is whether an embryo, unwanted by the woman who carries it, *should* be given the right to live and develop into a child, no matter how much this development damages the woman's interests.

We give a child the right to life. Until we have decided that we want also to give an embryo the very same right, unconditionally, we should not call it an *unborn child*, for that would prejudice inquiry.

5
THE INDISPENSABLE BACKSTOP

But why push abortion? Isn't birth control always preferable?

Let us grant that it is.

But does that mean that if all women use the best method of contraception we can get rid of abortion? Not at all: pills, diaphragms, condoms, foams, and IUDs can all fail.

Since the reason for using contraception is to avoid having a child at a particular time, when contraception fails, the woman still wants to avoid motherhood at that particular time. The term *birth control*, strictly speaking, means the prevention of births and includes abortion. In the total system of birth control, *abortion is the backstop* that corrects for contraceptive failure.

Is the backstop really needed?

The law, they say, is not concerned with trifles. Is contraceptive failure a trifling matter?

The most effective contraceptive method we have to date is the contraceptive pill. Its failure rate is approximately 1 percent. That is, if a hundred women use the pill faithfully for a year, one of them, on the average, will be pregnant before the year is out.

One percent? That's not much.

Oh, yes it is. There are about 54 million fertile women in the United States. About 3.5 million women bear a child during any given year. Let's assume that every one of these children is wanted. (This is certainly not true.) That leaves about 50 million women exposed to the risk of unwanted pregnancy each year.

If all these women use a contraceptive method that has a failure rate of 1 percent, how many unwanted conceptions will there be each year?

About half a million.

But at least a quarter—maybe a half—of these will be spontaneously aborted, most at so early an age that the mother isn't even sure she's pregnant before it's all over. Let's say half of them are spontaneously aborted. How many unwanted pregnancies to be carried to term does that leave?

A quarter of a million.

Conclusion: in a population the size of ours, the universal use of *the best method of contraception known generates a quarter of a million unwanted pregnancies per year.*

The calculation is only approximate, but it errs in underestimating the size of the need for abortion.

If the minipill is used, to minimize unwanted side effects, the failure rate rises to about 3 percent. That would produce three-quarters of a million unwanted births per year.

Other methods have even higher rates of failure. The worst is the rhythm method, which fails about 15 percent of the time. Reported effectiveness figures vary greatly for this method, depending on how many days are forbidden to intercourse. By restricting intercourse to a single day in the cycle, say the 27th, it can be quite effective.

Complete abstinence is still more effective. But not very popular.

Worst, of course, is intercourse without precautions. *But who would do such a thing?*

Lots of people.

Teenagers too shy to ask for help getting contraceptives, but unable to say no to Nature.

Neurotic people looking for trouble.

Ambivalent people, not sure what they want.

How many unwanted children are born each year in the United States? It depends on how you ask the question, and when you ask it. (Faced with the inevitable, a woman may talk herself into accepting it. The initially unwanted child may become a wanted child. Fortunately.)

The best estimate is that one-quarter of the children born alive in the United States are unwanted at the time of conception. That's about a million per year.

Before birth control, mandatory motherhood was the common fate of married women. And of many unmarried ones as well. A woman may have wanted a few of her children, but seldom did she want all of them.

Good contraception goes most of the way toward freeing women of unwanted motherhood, but it by no means frees them from the *fear* of it. This is a fact little realized by most men.

H. G. Wells tells us how he became educated to this truth when he read his mother's diary after her death. Her family was perpetually in need, and Mrs. Wells lived "in perpetual dread of further motherhood." Each month a sword of Damocles hung over her head. As the end of the intermenstrual period approached, her gnawing concern was, *Will I menstruate this time?*— That is, *Have I escaped pregnancy one more month?*

"Anxiety relieved" was the verbal formula by which this Victorian woman told her diary of one more escape from disaster. (But, several times, her anxiety was not relieved.)

Anxiety relieved. How much anxiety? How much justified?

Let's look at the mathematics of the situation: it may surprise you.

The probability of contraceptive success during an entire year for one woman may be as high as 99 percent. For some women. But for the total population, under real conditions, it is doubtful if the probability is, or is likely to be, higher than 97 percent. After all, we are human: we are neglectful, passionate beings.

If the probability of successfully avoiding pregnancy during one year's exposure to sexual intercourse is 97 percent, what is the probability that a woman will successfully avoid unwanted pregnancy for her thirty fertile years? It is 0.97 carried to the 30th power. This is only 40 percent.

Put the other way round: *Using a 97 percent perfect system of contraception a woman has a better than 50-50 chance of becoming unwantedly pregnant at least once in her lifetime.* In fact, the probability is 60 percent.

No method of contraception is perfect.

But the system of birth control that includes abortion *is* perfect.

No wonder women are fearful with contraception alone. Even if a woman never needs an abortion during her entire reproductive period, she does crave the psychological assurance that only the backstop of readily available abortion can give her.

6
MARGARET'S STORY

Is abortion needed? Statistics are essential in attacking such a question, but we need stories, too, to convey the human quality of the problem. The trouble is that there are too many stories. A million unwanted pregnancies, a million different stories. Some sort of selection has to be made.

In this chapter I will tell only one story. It is a true story, and rather extreme, but not uniquely so. To redress the balance I will, in the succeeding chapter, recount more ordinary stories.

This story is told in the woman's own words, without alteration. The time is about 1960. I will call the woman Margaret. She wrote:

> I had an illegal abortion 2½ years ago. I left my church because of the guilt I felt. I had six children when my husband left me to live with another

woman. We weren't divorced and I went to work to help support them. When he would come to visit the children he would sometimes stay after they were asleep. I became pregnant. When I told my husband, and asked him to please come back, he informed me that the woman he was living with was five months pregnant and ill, and that he couldn't leave her, not at that time anyway.

I got the name of a doctor in San Francisco from a Dr. friend who was visiting here from there. This Dr. (Ob. and Gyn.) had a good legitimate practice in the main part of the city and was a kindly, compassionate man who believes as you do, that it is better for everyone not to bring an unwanted child into the world.

It was over before I knew it. I thought I was just having an examination at the time. He even tried to make me not feel guilty by telling me that the long automobile trip had already started a spontaneous abortion. He charged me $25. That was on Fri. and on Mon. I was back at work. I never suffered any ill from it.

The other woman's child died shortly after birth and six months later my husband asked if he could come back. We don't have a perfect marriage but my children have a father. My being able to work has helped us out of a deep financial debt. I shall always remember the sympathy I received from that Dr. and wish there were more like him with the courage to do what they believe is right.

Any person of compassion cannot but feel sympathetic toward Margaret. But those who want, at all costs, to retain or reinstitute abortion prohibition have objections to make. We must listen to them.

Why didn't Margaret use contraceptives?

This is an interesting question, but an irrelevant one. We can't undo the past. Margaret is pregnant now: now what should she do?

If we let this woman have an abortion, others will be careless, as she was. We must make an example of her to deter others.

The same argument has been used for capital punishment. But criminologists are pretty well agreed that there is no positive evidence that capital punishment deters. (Capital punishment may or may not be justified on other grounds—that's not our question here.)

Why should we let a woman have an abortion just to satisfy her selfish desires? Mere convenience is no excuse.

Scolding others for selfishness is very popular. But is selfishness wholly wrong? Each of us is descended from an unbroken line of selfish individuals. Our ancestors thought enough of themselves to fight against "the slings and arrows of outrageous fortune." They survived. The utterly selfless ones were not our ancestors: they perished.

Besides: look again at Margaret's story. Is this the testimony of a very selfish woman? Do we not see here a great deal of loving concern for both husband and children? Note that Margaret was repelled by the thought of abortion, but she went ahead and had an abortion for the children's sake. Abortion was a loving gift to her family. Margaret saw her alternatives as these:

A. Abortion, leaving her with six children and a difficult but manageable situation. She could keep her job; she might be able to get her husband back; the children would have a father; they should be able to muddle along. Muddling along is often the best we can do in this life.

B. No abortion. Child No. 7 is born; Margaret loses her job; her husband likely throws in the sponge and disappears; the children lose a father; the mother, overworried, ends in a mental hospital, and the seven children are farmed out to foster parents. This is not a certain scenario, but it is a highly probable one.

So the options are these: six children tolerably well cared for versus seven miserably treated. Quality of life versus quantity. . . .

Margaret's choice: abortion for the children's sake.

She shouldn't have forgotten the contraceptives! She shouldn't have let her wandering husband get in bed with her! She shouldn't have had the first six children. She shouldn't have gotten married anyway.

Shouldn't . . . shouldn't . . . shouldn't—this is the disease of morality. We can't remake the past.

The moral question is: What do we do now?

7
PREGNANCY AS PUNISHMENT

I am not, basically, an activist. When I gave my first lecture on abortion, back in 1963, I intended it only as a calm, detached intellectual analysis, looking toward the eventual change in the law. I was certainly not offering my help in getting abortions for women. I can't be sure of my memory, but I don't think that I ever foresaw that my giving a public lecture would propel me into the role of an abortion counselor. (How naïve can one be?)

In any event, in less than twenty-four hours I had my first call for help: "Where can I get an abortion?" I didn't know, but when I heard her story I set about finding the answer. Other calls came in—by phone, by letter and in person—and for five years I was heavily involved in finding safe abortions for the unwillingly pregnant. It was not an occupation I would have chosen for myself, but it was the sort of call on one's conscience that one can't turn down.

Most of the hundreds of stories I heard were less spectacular, less heartrending than Margaret's. It is now time to redress the balance created by her story with two more ordinary cases.

A young unmarried couple (I will call them Anne and Michael) came to my office seeking help in arranging an abortion. They were both seniors in college, both biology students, and both had been admitted to medical school. Their academic records were excellent. He hoped to become an obstetrician; she a pediatrician. A good professional combination: the babies he delivered she would watch over. They weren't sure just when would be the best time to get married, but they planned to have two children after they were financially established.

Anne had just learned that she was pregnant. What of the future now? The probable alternatives were these:

A. Abortion. With luck and hard work, the scenario as planned before.

B. No abortion. Anne stops school, bears the baby, then has to go to work to support the child and help put Michael through school. There is a good chance she will never become a doctor. Or if she does, it will be at a much greater sacrifice, partly paid for by the child that was born at an inconvenient time.

They want children—but not yet.

Like Margaret, they want an abortion for the children's sake. But with them the abortion is for the sake of future children, the two children they hope to have later, children who will have a better chance in life if Anne and Michael postpone parenthood until they are financially better off.

Are they selfish? Is it selfish, is it contrary to society's interests, for a woman to want to be able to afford a child before she has one?

My last story is of a quite different sort of person. I will call her Juliette. From the moment she walked in the door I was repelled by her. If I were a good novelist I would be able to convey to the reader the repulsion she exuded; but I am not, and cannot.

Let me just say that the more she talked the more I was convinced that she was an utterly materialistic, utterly foolish, and completely self-centered person.

Well, you've made your bed, now lie in it—this is what I wanted to say to her. Fortunately I didn't. A stupider reaction to an unwanted pregnancy is hard to imagine. My assessment of Juliette's character may have been completely wrong. In that case my unspoken reaction to her was also wrong. But even if I was completely right in my judgment of Juliette, the proposal to punish with pregnancy is indefensible.

"You've made your bed, now lie in it"—whom are we punishing? The woman, certainly. But if the woman is as bad as we think, we are also punishing the child. What sort of justice is that?

And if the child is punished unjustly it will likely grow up twisted and pass some of the punishment on to society.

A good woman deserves to be released from unwanted pregnancy precisely because she is good.

A woman thought to be bad deserves this release even more—lest she punish those who are innocent of her wrongdoings and shortcomings, her child most of all.

In fact: is there any class of women for whom mandatory motherhood is to be recommended? Any group who will make the world a better place in which to live if they are compelled to bear children they don't want?

Listen with the psychoanalyst's "third ear" to those who want to use pregnancy as a punishment, and you will hear, loud and clear, the throttled voice of sexual envy.

Envy is a moral defect we all suffer from. The damage it does can be limited if we become acutely aware of the defect and the many camouflages it assumes.

The world isn't perfect. We can't get rid of all the suffering in the world. Sometimes it is precisely the suffering that ennobles a person, causing him (or her) to rise to new heights. Adversity builds character.

True.

But let us not forget what Mark Twain once said: "It is easy to bear adversity—another man's, I mean."

He would have been closer to the target had he finished his remark with these words: "when the adversity is borne by another person, I mean; especially if that other person is a woman."

8
THE TWO SUBCULTURES

When Justice Byron R. White dissented from the majority of the Supreme Court he condemned his brethren in law for their "improvident and extravagant . . . exercise of raw judicial power." The majority, as he saw it, held that "the Constitution of the United States values the convenience, whim or caprice of the putative mother more than the life or potential life of the fetus. . . ."

Putative mother? The father is always putative. ("It is a wise father that knows his own child," said Shakespeare.) Only the mother of a child or fetus is certain. Perhaps Justice White meant that we shouldn't speak of the woman who acts as host to a fetus as a mother until the fetus is born and becomes a baby? This is a defensible position, but an odd one to take if one opposes the majority decision of the Supreme Court, as Justice White did. But let it pass.

More significant are the words with which Justice White brushed off the interests of the "putative mother" by saying that mere *convenience, whim,* or *caprice* may lead a woman to request an abortion.

Sauce for the goose is sauce for the gander. Let's turn

the situation around a hundred and eighty degrees and look at it again. Let us imagine a court of law presided over by Judge Byron R. White.

The wife is the complainant. John and Mary Doe already have three children. John makes only $125 a week, but he is a careful manager, and the Does have no debts beyond the mortgage on the house and the time payments yet to be made on the car. Mary is light-headed and leaves everything up to John. Well, almost everything: religion is her department, and she believes it is her duty to have as many children "as God sends her." So when John takes to wearing condoms during intercourse she balks and hauls him into court. She asks that he be enjoined from using condoms.

"What do you have to say for yourself, John?" asks Judge White.

"It's all right here, Your Honor," says John, handing up his household accounts book. "After I've budgeted for all the necessities, $10 a month for vacations and entertainment, and $5 for unforeseen emergencies, there's not a cent left from my wages. If we have one more child, Your Honor, we'll have to go into debt. And how will we ever get out?"

The Judge scowls.

"That won't do," he says. "Your wife's desire for more and more children is eminently reasonable. At best, your actions are governed by mere *convenience*, whereas your wife's behavior springs from deep religious feelings. More likely, your attempts to avoid having more children spring from mere *whim* or *caprice*. The Court finds for the plaintiff and enjoins the further use of contraceptives."

Is that what Judge White would say to one of his own sex?

Not likely!

To the traditional-minded male only women indulge in whim or caprice; or, at their most rational, do things for mere convenience. Now as for a man—well, Shakespeare said it again, this time through the mouth of Hamlet: "What a piece of work is a man! how noble in reason! how infinite in faculty! in form and moving how express and admirable! in action how like an angel! in apprehension how like a god!"

Justice White would no doubt say, "Right on!" to this opinion.

One of the more subtle ideas of science is that of frames of reference. It is comparatively easy to discover new facts in science; but resolving a difficulty by uncovering hitherto unconscious frames of reference is more difficult. This is the sort of thing Einstein did. It is devilishly difficult. Our minds resist accepting new reference frames or even acknowledging the existence of old ones.

It was at a cocktail party. Abortion still was not a matter for polite conversation, but now that I had spoken out in public women spoke to me freely of their experiences. A middle-aged woman was telling me how she had been afraid it would be difficult to get an abortion in Catholic Italy (where she and her husband were staying for a while), only to discover that it was the easiest thing in the world.

When she finished her story I asked: "And what did you tell your husband?"

"Nothing," she replied calmly. "He's much too immature to think about such things."

I thought this amusing but didn't see the significance until I remembered what I had read years earlier about the Rif tribes of northern Africa.

Among the Rif, as with many people, abortion is a very serious offense—officially. If a man is certain that his wife has had an abortion he'll beat hell out of her, and nobody will protest. Does this mean that there are no abortions among Rif women? On the contrary: the women have no difficulty whatever in escaping unwanted pregnancies. Here's the way they do it.

In addition to the general market day, once a week there is a special market day for women only. Men are forbidden to enter. On the women's market day a woman can buy cosmetics, love potions, contraceptives—and abortion services. The men know nothing about it—officially. Unofficially they no doubt have their suspicions. But it would be a foolish man who tried to penetrate the secrets of the women's marketplace. That's her world; his lies outside.

So, of what significance is it that the Rif forbid abortions? Really very little. Rif *men* forbid abortions; Rif women *have* them.

In other words, the Rif culture is divided into two subcultures: the male subculture and the female subculture. With respect to abortion, one subculture creates the theory, and the other the practice. And scarcely the twain do meet.

(We would never have known of this if the male anthropologist who investigated the Rifs had not taken his wife along. Think how much we must have overlooked in "primitive" cultures because male anthropologists visited them by themselves.)

It isn't just primitive cultures that are divided into two subcultures: ours is too. And the division used to be much deeper than it is now. For hundreds of years women's medical needs were taken care of mostly by other women. Particularly their reproductive needs. Midwives, until recently, were just what the name implies: women. They not only delivered babies; they also ministered to menstrual troubles, gave advice on contraceptives, and performed abortions. All this was within the confidential confines of the female subculture; men knew little of it.

Even today, in much of Europe, midwives take charge of most reproductive matters. The nominal religion of the country seems to be almost without effect on what women do in the womanly areas. Because the male-controlled legal apparatus interferes with the distribution of good contraceptives, the need for, and practice of, abortion is greater in Catholic countries than it is in Protestant. Men write the laws; women do what is needful.

The disparity between male laws and female practice is nowhere more evident than in Italy. Italy's population is just a quarter of that of the United States, but the 53rd Congress of Obstetrics and Gynecology held in Bologna in 1968 estimated that there were 3,000,000 abortions per year, all illegal and officially immoral, of course. If that is true, the Italian rate per unit population is twelve times the rate usually estimated for the United States before abortion was legalized. A million per year was the usual estimate. Of course, illegal operations are always difficult to estimate, but the figure of 1.6 million legal abortions (see "mourning box" in chapter 1) per year since legalization of abortion in the United States suggests that the former estimate could not have been far wrong.

In any case, it is crystal clear that ethical theory in the male subculture in Italy has little effect on practice in the female subculture.

Once your mind rearranges its facts in the reference frame of two subcultures you can never again take seriously the writings of men who knew only of the male subculture. I refer to the male theologians and the male moralists who are usually cited as *the* moral authorities. In their minds there is only one culture—*the* culture —*man's* culture, where *man* alternately means all of humankind and the male of the species only. The implied reference to *man* vibrates back and forth between the two meanings like one of those optical illusions that can be seen either of two ways and won't stay put.

There were no laws against abortion until the nineteenth century, but many men maintain that the moral condemnation of abortion is centuries old. They point to the works of Saint Augustine, Tertullius and Saint Thomas Aquinas.

Every one of the "authorities" is a man.

Every one of them lived within the male subculture and was blissfully unaware that there was any other.

"The judgment of God upon your sex endures even today; and with it inevitably endures your position of criminal at the bar of justice. You are the gateway of the devil"—Tertullian, speaking to womankind generally.

"A woman should be covered with shame by the thought she is a woman"—Clement of Alexandria.

Augustine, Bishop of Hippo, in one of his kindlier moments said: "Despise not yourselves, ye women; the Son of God was born of woman."

Such were the men who created the literature that from time immemorial condemned abortion.

How can one take this male-oriented literature seriously? It is as though iguanas in the middle of the desert were to write treatises on the life that flourishes in the depths of the sea.

9
THE COMMUNITY'S INTEREST

Be a bleeding heart if you want to, but I can tell you where I stand with respect to women. It's dog eat dog in this world, and I don't give a hoot about your silly, complaining broads. If a woman gets pregnant that's no skin off my nose. She's made her bed, now let her lie in it. No abortion for her—not at my expense. I'm looking out for Number One.

A defensible position, if not a noble one. It would be useless to ask the speaker to be less selfish and more interested in the welfare of others. We must take his statement at face value and see what attitude an unashamed and thorough egotist should have toward abortion.

Sweden made abortion legal in 1939—legal, but very difficult to get. Figuratively speaking, a woman had to come crawling on her knees to a committee (dominated by men) which would decide if she had a sufficient "excuse" for an abortion. Much testimony was heard, and voluminous documents placed on file. Reinvestigations were often called for. Quite frequently, the decision was postponed from one meeting to the next. And the next. And. . . .

In the meantime the woman was more and more pregnant. She grew ever bigger. She began to feel the embryo stir in her uterus. In her mind the embryo became less a thing and more a child-to-be.

The committee's decision often came so late that she decided to go through with the childbirth, even when the committee was favorable. (No doubt this was the goal the delaying action was designed to achieve.)

Quite often the committee said No. Then what? Some women went abroad for their abortions. Some aborted themselves.

Some died.

And some had babies. Unwanted babies. Unwanted at the time of conception. (No doubt a few women were blessedly able to rationalize a desire for that which they could not escape.)

So what? Does it matter whether a baby is wanted or not, once it's born?

Beginning in 1960 Hans Forssman and Inga Thuwe sought to find the answer. They searched out the children born after their mothers requested, and were denied, abortions. These children were, then, unwanted at the time of pregnancy. They were now twenty-one years old. How had they made out? To answer this question with confidence a control group was needed for comparison.

Forssman and Thuwe assembled their control group

from young people of the same age who had been born to mothers who had *not* requested abortion. They were presumed wanted. They came from the same socioeconomic background and were born in the same hospitals.

The full results are presented in Appendix C; what follows here is only a brief summary. The differences between study and control groups were statistically significant. Simply stated, they were as follows:

As compared with the control group, unwanted children—

1. were in poorer health;
2. had histories of more psychiatric care;
3. used alcohol more;
4. if boys, had been more consistently rejected by the army;
5. and if girls, had themselves become mothers at a younger age.

What does all this mean to the John Q. Citizen who unashamedly says he is concerned only about himself? The meaning is surely obvious.

Like it or not, we all live in a welfare state now. To an ever-greater extent we are all taxed to pay for the ill health of others. Even a thoroughly selfish man must be concerned about laws that diminish the mental and physical health of the young. He must also view with alarm anything that starts people down the road to alcoholism, because he'll pay for that too. Girls who have babies while they're very young are more likely to end up on welfare. His taxes pay for welfare, too.

The critical reader of Forssman and Thuwe's paper

in Appendix C may well come up with objections like the following:

"How can you think of basing policy on so small a sample? After all, there were only a hundred and twenty children in each group. And this was in Sweden, which is certainly different from the United States. The cultures are different. Before we do anything, shouldn't we wait until we've carried out a similar controlled study here, using thousands of subjects?"

The proposal is plausible, but close examination shows it to be unreasonable.

First of all, it would be virtually impossible to repeat the experiment in the United States now. Sweden had a system that was uniquely well suited to such a study (though it was hard on women): it was possible though difficult to get a legal abortion. This made it easy to find a study group later. It would be difficult to find such a group here because we have moved rapidly from no permissions for legal abortion to essentially freely available permissions.

If we waited for such a study here, that would mean we would have to refuse abortions to some women now and then wait for a bit more than twenty-one years plus nine months to assemble our study group. It would be nearly the year 2000 before we would have results we could base policy on. In the meantime, what about all the women? Would they passively accept the fate imposed on them?

And what about the millions of unwanted children born? Must we regard their suffering as the price of objectivity?

The basic error in the demand that we wait for U.S.

data before doing anything is the belief that we can do nothing in the meantime. Doing nothing in this case—refusing legal abortions—is being responsible for something like a million unwanted births (or illegal abortions) per year.

The Forssman and Thuwe study, small as it is, is all that we have, and all that we are ever likely to have. Its uniqueness is a major reason for reprinting it here. Asking for more and larger studies before taking action is misplaced objectivity.

"Life," said Samuel Butler, "is the art of drawing sufficient conclusions from insufficient premises."

Those who are sensitive to the needs of others are touched by the needless suffering mandatory motherhood adds to the lot of mothers and children. Those who care not a fig for mothers and children—or who say they don't—should nevertheless be disturbed that some of the economic cost of mandatory motherhood falls on them as taxpayers.

The most surprising thing about hard-headed, selfish people is not their selfishness. That has an easy evolutionary explanation: natural selection favors it. (In fact, it is altruism—which is also real—that challenges the explanatory power of the theory of evolution most severely.)

The most surprising thing about selfish people is how often they are obstinately blind to their own true self-interest. In 1973, while waiting for their various mandatory-motherhood amendments to work their way through congressional committees, the Right-to-Lifers introduced a spate of bills and riders designed to hamstring legal abortion. For instance, Senator James Buckley introduced an amendment to the Social Security bill which denied Medicaid funds for abortion. In practice, this would mean a return to the pre-1960 system of good abortions for the rich and lousy ones—or none—for the poor. Under such a system, poor women who get incompetent abortions (perhaps self-induced) have a high rate of infection by disease and, with a high probability—

1. they end up in the hospital, on public funds, and/or
2. they die, in which case:
   a. their burial has to be paid for by taxpayers, and
   b. their already born children, now orphaned, may well have to be taken care of at taxpayers' expense.

And, if they don't get abortions, they bear children, which make the mothers even less capable of taking care of themselves financially.

Who benefits by mandatory motherhood for the poor? Certainly not the poor. And just as certainly not the rich. Yet the Senators, who no doubt pride themselves on being realistic, accepted the amendment and voted a new Social Security bill which would, if put into effect, increase the need for more Social Security in the future.

"The rich get richer and the poor get children."

Much more legislation like this and only the second half of the aphorism will be true. We can live with selfish men—but God protect us from *blind* and selfish men.

"She's made her bed, now let her lie in it." But did she make that bed by herself? In a welfare state we all must lie in it.

10
THE SIXTH COMMANDMENT

"Thou shalt not kill." Such is the Sixth Commandment. What does it mean?

A few Christians, like Albert Schweitzer, say—or imply—that we shouldn't kill any living thing. "Reverence for life." But it is impossible to follow this rule. We kill untold billions of bacteria whenever we chlorinate our drinking water. Since a small fraction of the bacteria may be lethal disease-producers, "it's them or us." We prefer to kill them.

And Albert Schweitzer smashed spiders with gusto.

A less extreme interpretation of the commandment in Exodus 20 is that it means "Thou shalt not kill human beings." But if this interpretation is correct, how are we to explain the religious fervor with which the Hebrews killed their enemies? In this they were encouraged, and even aided, by the Lord.

Evidently "Thou shalt not kill" is not an absolute commandment. The apparent inconsistency of the Bible disappears when we consult a more accurate translation. The wording just given is that of the Douay Version of the Bible (Roman Catholic), published in 1610, and the King James Version (Protestant), published in 1611. But translations made in this century, truer to the original texts, render the Sixth Commandment thus:

"Thou shalt not commit murder."

Murder is a question of definition; a matter of interpretation, a question of choice in the use of words. A murder is an unapproved killing. So the Sixth Commandment raises this question: What killings are approved, or permissible?

Killing an enemy in war?
Killing a traitor in peacetime?
Killing a murderer (capital punishment)?
Killing to save one's own life?
Killing an aggressor to prevent the murder of the innocent?

In all these cases we are confronted with—

1. a fully human being, usually a legal adult; and
2. a question of guilt or innocence.

Opinions differ as to when it is permissible to kill a guilty adult. It is almost universally agreed that it is never permissible to kill an innocent adult. And some people say no adult should ever be killed, innocent or not. Weighing their arguments is not our business here.

We are concerned here not with adults but with very early embryos. Should it be permissible to kill them?

Right-to-Lifers argue that an embryo's life must not be taken *because the embryo is innocent*. In what sense? For there are two senses in which we use the word *innocent*.

First, a person may be innocent of a crime if he has had a chance to commit it and has refrained from doing so. This is the most impressive kind of innocence. Punishing this kind of innocence seems inappropriate and unjust.

Secondly, a person or object is innocent of all the crimes it had no chance to commit. I am innocent of President Kennedy's murder, as is also the petunia in my garden. But I may indeed be suffering some of the consequences of his murder, innocent or not. Is my innocence (or the petunia's) of any real consequence?

The word *innocence* is ambiguous. The Right-to-Life position capitalizes on this ambiguity. Is the question of innocence relevant to the abortion problem? Some Right-to-Lifers doubt it. The issue divides the group, as the following example shows.

Occasionally a woman has an ectopic pregnancy—a pregnancy that is literally out of (the normal) place. The embryo may implant, for example, on the wall of a fallopian tube instead of in the uterus. If the embryo continues to grow in the wrong place it may kill the mother. Is it permissible to kill (and remove) the embryo before this happens, thus saving the life of the woman?

Some Right-to-Lifers say no. The embryo is innocent and cannot be killed. It is this school of thought that is embodied in the proposed Hogan Amendment, quoted in the first chapter.

Other Right-to-Lifers are unwilling to sacrifice the woman. Their position is incorporated in the Buckley Amendment, also proposed in 1973. Section 2 reads: "This article shall not apply in an emergency when a reasonable medical certainty exists that continuation of the pregnancy will cause the death of the mother."

Those Right-to-Lifers who agree with this decision, but who are also hung up on the concept of innocence, justify the killing of the embryo in an ectopic pregnancy in the following way. The continued development threatens the mother's life. Therefore, the embryo is really an aggressor. An aggressor is by definition not innocent. Therefore, the embryo's life may be taken to save the innocent mother. The argument is ingenious, but many people think such a bending of words goes beyond the elastic limit of language.

Suppose we grant that an "innocent" embryo-out-of-place in the fallopian tube can be killed to save the woman who carries it (who is certainly innocent of positioning it). Then can we ethically kill an embryo that is out of place *economically* speaking, if there are insufficient funds to raise it properly?

Is it all right to kill an embryo that is *psychologically* out of place in the uterus of a woman who is going crazy with ten kids already?

What if the embryo is *temporally* out of place because it has been conceived too soon in the life plans of the prospective parents?

This graded sequence of cases hints at what some moralists call the danger of the "thin edge of the wedge." Let us look now at this classic problem.

11
THE THIN EDGE OF THE WEDGE

Way back in 1920, when birth control was a shocking topic, sex was still more shocking. And most shocking of all was the discussion of sex technique by a woman.

But that didn't stop Marie Stopes.

This English woman's *Married Love* was a runaway best seller. By today's standards it was pretty timid stuff, but a male moralist of the time, one W. N. Willis, detected dangerous "tendencies" in this sex manual. To Mrs. Stopes's suggestion that it was quite all right for a wife to embrace her husband with her legs as well as with her arms, the moralist, aghast, protested that such stimulants to passion "ordinarily do not enter the head of a normal woman." We must, Willis wrote,

> in the name of true, normal manhood and womanhood, and indeed the name of the British Empire, endeavour to keep the imagination down at all costs—never purposely call it into play, as suggested by Mrs. Stopes. . . . The imagination should . . . be subdued on all sides, and on every possible occasion, when sex is being considered, for the human imagination is the most deadly foe to the clean, wholesome methods of Nature. . . . Insidious advocacy of birth control is but *the thin edge of the wedge* for undermining the institution of marriage and securing a state of lawless love. (Italics added.)

The thin edge may not be horrible in itself: it is the thick wedge presumed to be following it that evokes fear. Willis did not say that embracing with the legs was immoral in itself. What he feared was the downfall of the British Empire—a thought which should give pause to every passionate wife in bed with her English husband!

This was neither the first nor the last time the argument of the wedge has been invoked.

When George III, during a time of wheat shortage, thought to set an example by giving up the powdering of his hair with flour, some of Pitt's men protested that he was undermining the distinction between the classes, which would lead to anarchy.

When Sir John Lubbock put forward a parliamentary bill that would reduce the hours of work to twelve on weekdays and fourteen on Saturday—this was in 1888—critics said he had opened the door to further legislation "of the most terrible character."

When evolutionists said that the "primal pair," Adam and Eve, were purely mythical, Victorian critics retorted that to admit this would bring on a chaos like that in the late Roman Empire, and the British people would soon have "no laws, no worship, and no property. . . . Society must fall to pieces if Darwinism be true."

When Matthew Arnold proposed to eliminate the prohibition against marriage with deceased wife's sister, his opponents said that doing so would open the door to bigamy, polygamy, and what Gladstone had described as "the more horrible forms of incest."

And when, in our own time, men and women concerned with the well-being of women propose that mandatory motherhood be brought to a close (which can only be done if hundreds of thousands of embryos are killed and aborted each year), some people with deep moral concerns have cried, *Auschwitz! Buchenwald!*

It's the thin edge of the wedge argument, of course.

The danger is not completely unreal. We must take it seriously.

If only we can find a solution that is *not* a part of a

wedge, a time when pregnancy can be stopped *before life begins*. . . .

12
WHEN DOES LIFE BEGIN?

Before 1800, the law in European cultures was indifferent to abortion. Then gradually during the nineteenth century one nation after another enacted abortion-prohibition laws. Why the change?

As a historical matter, we don't know the answer. The historical investigations are yet to be made. A number of plausible causes can be suggested. First, the two subcultures—male and female—were growing together somewhat. In the upper reaches of society, women were gaining a little political and social power. The "commerce between the sexes," to use an antique phrase, was not all transacted in bed. The first fighters for women's rights appeared in the late eighteenth century, and their numbers increased during the nineteenth.

Second, male physicians began ministering to women, at least among the upper classes. Male midwives—a paradoxical name—began to appear. Were they shocked at what they learned of abortion? Certainly none of their male patients had ever asked to be aborted.

Third, in the pre-antiseptic, pre-anesthetic days all operations were pretty dangerous. Many operations were outlawed in some places. Perhaps abortion was seen as merely one more dangerous operation.

Whatever the explanation, by the latter half of the nineteenth century abortions were outlawed throughout most of Europe and in Europe-derived cultures like our own. But in spite of the laws, abortions—even legal abortions—continued. How come?

The abortions women were getting in the late nineteenth century were usually not *called* abortions because they occurred before quickening. Around the sixteenth to eighteenth week—the time isn't precise—a pregnant woman for the first time feels the embryo moving. She quickens, as the old expression puts it. From that moment on, she knows she has a live "child" inside her.

What about before quickening? People weren't sure.

Either what was there was not a child;

Or it was not alive;

Or it was in some state intermediate between life and death—a sort of biological limbo.

In any case, the time of quickening made a convenient point for drawing a line between permissible and nonpermissible intervention in pregnancy. The line allowed two different ways of referring to intervention:

Intervention before quickening was called "bringing the period on."

Intervention after quickening was called "abortion."

Under that convenient distinction what we now call abortions were legally performed in prohibition states well into the twentieth century, before practice finally caught up with biological knowledge gained in the nineteenth.

Many people thought that bringing the period on was not a killing because "it" was not yet alive. Life had not yet begun, they thought. Even today, women midwives continue to carry out early abortions among the lower classes in Europe under this psychologically protective semantic umbrella.

They are wrong, of course.

When does life begin?
The true answer is simple: *Never.*

That answer may not be satisfactory to disturbed legislators looking desperately for a way to manage abortions, but it is the only true answer. Life no doubt did begin once, many years ago. Archbishop Ussher, the Irishman who put the dates between the columns of the King James Version of Genesis, thought that the world—hence life—began in 4004 B.C. Darwinians think it began about three billion years ago. Began once only. *In our experience* life never begins. Life is just passed on from one cell to another.

Life ends—often.

Life begins—never. Not so far as we can see.

If life did begin easily, time after time, we'd be in a pickle. When we preserve food in cans we heat the cans to kill all the living bacteria in them. When a can cools down, it is a splendid place for living organisms to flourish. But they don't, for two reasons. First, they can't get in. Second, living things are never spontaneously generated out of nonliving. We've been sure of this for almost a hundred years now, because of the splendid work of Louis Pasteur and John Tyndall.

Life doesn't spring up spontaneously in canned foods. No more does it do so in the human uterus. How odd it is, then, to read the cautious language of Justice Blackmun in the majority opinion of the Supreme Court. He says:

> We need not resolve the difficult question of when life begins. When those trained in the respective disciplines of medicine, philosophy, and theology, are unable to arrive at any consensus, the judiciary, at this point in the development of man's knowledge, is not in a position to speculate. . . .

From subsequent remarks, it appears that he really means to ask, "At what point in development shall we call this thing human?" But he fails to make this quite proper question explicit.

As for the question, "When does life begin?" *all* biologists (and, I should think, all medical men) are in agreement on the answer: *never*. Any other opinions philosophers and theologians may have are not supported by facts.

That Justice Blackmun throws a murky net over the issue should not be regarded as his fault (for most of his fellow jurists are no better). At fault is the educational system which has allowed lawyers to grow up in essential ignorance of some of the most important facts of biology. We've known for a hundred years that life never begins. But apparently we did not tell this to the students in our law schools.

In the human life cycle, a living sperm cell from the male unites with a living egg cell of the female. The resulting fertilized egg (or zygote) is also alive.

The living zygote divides into two living cells.

These two living cells divide into four living cells.

Four to eight . . ,

Eight to sixteen . . .
And so on.
All alive.
Life never begins.

There is no way to eliminate mandatory motherhood if we forbid the killing of human cells. There is no time in the life cycle of human beings "before life begins." Either we must perpetuate mandatory motherhood—or we must reconcile ourselves to killing human cells.

If the latter, we must develop some philosophy for distinguishing between the stages of human development with respect to permissible and nonpermissible killing. A Right-to-Life Amendment would assert that all killings of embryos are nonpermissible. What would be the ultimate consequences of adopting this position?

Let's see.

13
TRUTH'S DAY IN COURT

"Your Honor. My client has been accused of murder under the Twenty-eighth Amendment to the Constitution of the United States. There is no argument as to the facts, so I ask that the Court look deeper into the meaning of those facts.

"My client, Dr. Samaritan, is a profoundly compassionate man. His behavior on the witness stand, I am sure, convinced everyone of this. As Margaret's physician he was deeply touched when this unfortunate woman came to him with her problem. Six children already; and now impregnated with a seventh by a husband who had left home to live with another woman— whom he had also made pregnant. No financial reserves.

A job that barely supported her family; and that job would be lost if she went through with the pregnancy and childbirth.

"What man of compassion and imagination could fail to be touched by the poor woman's plight? Dr. Samaritan is rich in both compassion and imagination. And courage. So he performed the simple operation the woman desired, and a family was saved from disaster.

"I will not base my argument on a peculiarity found in the enforcement of all abortion-prohibition laws, but I cannot refrain from mentioning it in passing. Abortion, it is said, is a crime. Distinguishing between the principal and the accessory to a crime as we do in law, who is the principal in the 'crime' of abortion? Clearly the woman. It is she who wills the crime.

"Who is the accessory? Clearly the physician who commits the crime at the woman's request. He is in her employ.

"Who is punished? Only the accessory, the physician. Never the principal.

"In one hundred years of abortion-prohibition in the United States never once has the principal—the woman herself—been punished for the crime of abortion. Threatened, yes. Badgered by the police, yes. They want to make her reveal the name of the accessory. But the woman is never punished.

"What kind of a crime is it for which we punish only the accessory to the crime and never the principal? Could it be—I don't say that it is—but just could it be that we don't believe, deep in our hearts, that abortion *is* a crime? What other explanation can there be for our odd conduct?

"But I said I would not linger over this peculiarity of the law. I have a much more fundamental issue to explore with the Court."

Mr. Sequitur, Margaret's attorney—a pudgy little man—mopped his florid face with a silk handkerchief and strolled back to his table. On cue, his assistant lifted a box from the floor, a box big enough to hold an inflated basketball. Sequitur, placing his hand on the top, turned to the judge.

"If you will permit it, Your Honor, I have a little demonstration for the Court." He turned again to the box and very deliberately untied and opened it. He reached in and started to draw something out. A hush had fallen over the courtroom. All eyes were on the lawyer's hands. Sequitur, sensing the tension, thoughtfully removed his hands from the box and turned to the judge again.

"Before I go on with the demonstration, I must prepare the ground. You know that it is possible to transplant a fertilized egg from the womb of one woman to the womb* of another. In this way it is sometimes possible to bring the blessings of motherhood to a woman who would otherwise be fruitless. This is a fine thing, but unfortunately it is difficult to get the fertilized egg in just the right condition for transplanting it into another womb.

"Sterility specialists have long recognized that what is really needed is a way of nourishing and maintaining

---

* He means *uterus*, of course; but considering the time and the place, Mr. Sequitur is probably wise to lapse into poetry.

a woman's ovaries in the laboratory, in 'tissue culture,' as they call it. This is easier said than done. Thousands of man-hours have gone into this work, without success.

"Today it is my great privilege to announce, for the first time in public, magnificent success in this humanitarian effort. The official announcement will appear in the *New England Journal of Medicine* next month. I am proud to say that it is scientists in our own Huxley University, led by the brilliant Dr. Bokanovsky, who have achieved this stunning success.

"Dr. Bokanovsky's group have found how to maintain a female ovary indefinitely in a culture apparatus in the laboratory. More: they have learned how to stimulate an ovary so that it will turn out eggs at a rate close to that at which a testicle turns out spermatozoa. Putting eggs and spermatozoa together they produce fertilized eggs ready for implanting in the waiting wombs of women yearning for motherhood. The Fertility Laboratory of Huxley University is now prepared to make every woman in the world happy with her very own baby. We may confidently expect the Nobel Prize to be awarded for this great accomplishment."

Sequitur paused and drank some water from a glass. Turning again to the bench, he continued.

"Dr. Bokanovsky, learning of this trial, has very generously lent me some of his material. I have here in this flask"—Sequitur reached into the box and pulled out a two-liter Erlenmeyer flask with a plastic cap on it—"a suspension of living human eggs, all fertilized and ready to be transplanted into expectant mothers."

The attorney sloshed the liquid around in the half-filled flask. The fluid was milky and just slightly pink. Sequitur paced back and forth, thoughtfully jiggling the flask as he walked.

"How many fertilized eggs do you suppose there are in here? Dr. Bokanovsky has carefully sampled this flask and made the calculations. There are, he tells me, two times ten to the thirteenth fertilized eggs in this little vessel. In numbers more familiar to most of us— certainly to me—that's twenty trillion. That sounds like a lot. How many is it? What can we compare this large number with?

"I think our best course is to compare it with the total number of people *who have ever lived* on this old planet of ours. Twenty years ago the demographer Nathan Keyfitz calculated that this was 77 billion. With the continued burgeoning of the population I am told that this number stands today at 80 billion. That is, all the people who have ever lived, amount to only 80 billion.

"According to the Twenty-eighth Amendment every fertilized egg is a human being, in the full meaning of the law. *I have, then, in this flask, twenty trillion human beings—two hundred and fifty times as many as have ever lived before on earth*. Now—"

Sequitur removed the lid.

"Now—"

Quickly he inverted the flask and with a swinging motion sprayed the contents in a semicircular swath on the floor. The audience gasped. The judge, his mouth open, half rose to admonish the attorney, but Sequitur, his voice loud and insistent, continued rapidly, precluding interruption.

"Bear with me! Bear with me! I know I have sullied

the dignity of this courtroom, but I will make amends. Bear with me! My argument is far more serious than any minor disorder I may have created.

"A moment ago this flask had twenty trillion living human beings in it. Now they are spread out all over this courtroom floor. They are still alive. But they won't be for long. The most heroic efforts we could possibly mount would not save them now. They will die.

"And who killed them? *I* killed them. I, John Sequitur, killed them! In front of your very eyes, I have killed two hundred and fifty times as many people as have ever lived on earth. Adolf Hitler and Genghis Khan were pikers compared to me. I, John Sequitur, am the greatest murderer of all time.

"The law, it has been said, does not concern itself with trifles. My client snuffed out the life of *one* human embryo. The Twenty-eighth Amendment says that every woman's embryo is a human being from the moment of conception, and that my client is a murderer. I, my client's attorney, have just snuffed out the lives of twenty trillion human beings. So says the Twenty-eighth Amendment.

"Do not concern yourself with trifles, Your Honor. Release my client—and charge *me* with murder. Mass murder."

14

WHO IS RESPONSIBLE? AND FOR WHAT?

It takes imagination to see the truth. Do Right-to-Lifers have enough imagination?

We should never pass a law unless we are convinced that it will be good not just for today, but for many years to come. The environment in which laws must be judged is now dominated by technology. Technology, as everyone knows, changes at a rapid pace. And the pace accelerates.

But the law changes at a snail's pace. It always has. By the time we get an amendment to the Constitution passed and ratified, the technological environment may be so changed that the law is no good—if, indeed, it ever was.

The attempt to predict what the future holds for us is called "technology assessment." One of its most powerful tools is science fiction. Science fiction arouses the imagination and helps it to see the truth. The probable truth, on which prudent men base their actions.

How probable is it that we shall some day culture human ovaries in the laboratory? Highly probable. Tissue culture—the growing of cells or groups of cells called tissues—is fiendishly complicated; but in principle all tissue-culture problems are soluble. Every tissue lives in an environment of nourishing fluid. No other tissue directly takes care of it—just the fluid produced by other tissues, and the fluid is not alive. We should be able to figure out what's in it, and furnish a similar fluid to tissues in a culture flask.

Tissue culture of human ovaries is probably "just around the corner." We would be fools to pass a law that did not allow for this probable technological development. That is the message of the story of John Sequitur in tomorrow's courtroom.

Splattering twenty trillion living human embryos on a courtroom floor is a rather violent way to make a point. Sequitur could have made it another way. A way that might have been better from an intellectual point of view, though probably not as effective in a courtroom.

Let's turn the film back to the point just before the lawyer emptied the flask on the floor. Only this time he doesn't empty it. Instead. . . .

"Your Honor," Sequitur says, "since this court is bound to uphold the law there can be no question about its attitude toward the life of these twenty trillion little beings. The Twenty-eighth Amendment says that each and every one of them is a human being in the full sense of the law. The honorable court must, then, cherish the life of each and every one. To willfully kill even one would be murder. Even to allow one to die from neglect would be manslaughter.

"They don't look like human beings. But the Twenty-eighth Amendment says they are."

Sequitur walks toward the bench, saying as he approaches it: "Dr. Bokanovsky gave them to me—"

He stretches upward and puts the flask on the bench: "—and I give them to you."

He coughs.

"Bokanovsky is through with them. I'm through with them. Now what are you going to do with them, Your Honor?

"Their lives can be continued if each of them is placed in the welcoming womb of a healthy woman. How many of them can be taken care of this way? At the outside there are, in the world, one billion women of childbearing age who might conceivably—pardon the pun—act as havens for these little beings. So out of every twenty thousand fertilized eggs in this flask only one can be saved by placing it in some woman's womb. (Even that would be practically impossible, considering how widely scattered these women are over the globe. And what makes us think they would all welcome such a gift?)

"But granting that the practical problem could be solved, for every fertilized egg you saved, 19,999 would have to die.

"And neither you, nor I, nor Dr. Bokanovsky—nor anybody else—can do a thing about it."

Sequitur takes a drink of water before going on.

"The trouble is, Your Honor, the assumptions of the law are back end to. We are deceived by language. We speak of 'conceiving life' or 'creating life,' when we can do neither. The life of existing cells can merely be continued in new individuals, in new *loci*, as it were. Imprisoned in ancient presumptions, we think it is difficult to 'create' life, and easy to continue it.

"The truth is quite the reverse. The so-called creation of life is childishly simple, and indeed much of this creation is done by those who are little more than children in the level of their understanding. Any two fools of the opposite sex can procreate another child, another life, as we say. It is the continuance and nourishing of life that is tragically difficult. Fools can—and do—create more life than the wisest and most powerful men and women in the world can possibly take care of.

"You can't possibly save more than the tiniest fraction of those lives in the flask before you. The vast majority will soon die. Will *you* then be responsible for the trillions of deaths? Or will *I* who gave these fertilized eggs to you be responsible? Or will *Bokanovsky*, who created them (as we say), be the responsible party?

"If we feel a compulsion to find and label a crime, what is that crime?

"Does the crime reside in the early destruction of these surplus lives, not wanted by anyone?

"Or is it the creation of lives for which there is no place in the world that constitutes the true crime?

"Or is it an error to think that there *is* a crime? Maybe both the so-called creation of new lives and their destruction at an early stage are completely without moral significance?

"Maybe the mistake is in looking for a crime at this stage of the life cycle. God knows we have more than enough to do trying to patch up the broken and spoiled lives of millions of human beings in the years after birth. Why, in heaven's name, do we anguish over these little eggs and embryos?

"Is mere life so precious? Or should our abiding concern be for the quality of life?"

15
HOW VALUABLE IS INFORMATION?

A fertilized human egg is about 130 microns in diameter. In a strong light it is just barely visible to the naked eye. It seems to have little structure in it, even when studied with an ordinary light microscope; though the electron microscope shows that it possesses a good deal of "fine structure." But there certainly isn't anything even remotely like an adult man or woman in it.

Yet everything that is needed to produce an adult

human being is there, in the chromosomes which are inside the nucleus which is inside the cell.

The adult *is* there—but only in a *potential* sense.

In the sense that the pattern of a rug is present in the punched cards that guide the loom.

In the sense in which the sound of your voice is present in the fluctuations of the electric current in the telephone wire.

In the sense in which a colored picture is present in the invisible waves created in the "ether" by a TV transmitter.

What is in the fertilized egg is *information*—information for creating the adult structure, if this cell and its derived cells are suitably fed and cared for. The potential then becomes actual. And the information in the nucleus of the zygote is identical with the information in the nuclei of the cells of the adult derived from it.*

This identity of information has been used by Right-to-Lifers to bolster the opinion they had already reached by other means. Since a zygote has all the information it needs to produce an adult human being, it *is* a human being, they say. Though posing as a statement of fact, this is really a personal judgment. Is it a wise judgment? Should we accept *identity of information* as the overwhelming criterion on which to base the ethical and legal decisions involved in abortion?

How valuable is information? Let us seek general principles in a less emotional situation.

* Those who know quite a bit of modern biology will know of some interesting exceptions to this blunt statement; but a moment's thought will show that these are not relevant to the problems treated here, so they are ignored hereafter.

HOW VALUABLE IS INFORMATION?

A man is about to build a house that will cost $50,000. As he stands on the site looking at the blueprints a practical joker comes along and sets fire to the blueprints. Question: Can the owner go to court and collect $50,000 for his lost blueprints?

The answer is obvious: No. If another set of blueprints will cost $10, that's what the court will award him. (Maybe a bit more for his time; perhaps even a bit for "mental anguish.")

Conclusion: *the value of replaceable information is the cost of its replacement.*

The principle applies equally to blueprints for houses and "blueprints" for living beings, which is what the chromosomes of a nucleus amount to.

Potential value is different from actual value.

To turn a $10 set of blueprints into a $50,000 house you have to pour in something like $50,000 worth of labor and materials.

To turn a microscopic set of chromosomal blueprints into a decent human being, you have to pour in a lot of labor and materials—*and love*. If you are short any of the necessary ingredients, why hang onto embryonic structures that are scarcely more than blueprints? Potential is not actual; it takes work to make it so.

No one is so foolish as to call a set of blueprints a house.

Why should we call a tiny embryo a human being?

The farther along a living being is in the developmental process—the more nearly potential has become actual—the more valuable that being is, by any rational standard of value.

Despite what Right-to-Lifers say, not all stages of

existence are equally valuable. The early stages have much less actual value. This is not only a rational conclusion; it is also what all ordinary persons, what "artizans, countrymen and merchants" (to use the language of Thomas Sprat) know. Their wives know it even better.

You know it, too.

A simple thought-experiment shows that this is so.

Suppose you were to notice a young woman weeping most of the time. On inquiring, you learn that six months earlier her child had been taken by death.

You ask: "How old was it?"

Consider what your reaction would be to the following two possible answers.

First possible answer: "It was ten years old." Wouldn't your immediate response be one of sympathy? In the end you might try to get her to pull herself together and start making new life. But you would feel that her present sorrow was quite understandable.

Second possible answer: "The 'child' was a six-week-old embryo."

How much sympathy would you feel in this case? Six months later, and she's still weeping? She should see a psychiatrist! (After all she can get pregnant again.)

The actions of all normal, loving women are consistent with the view that embryos are not nearly so valuable as children several years old. The grief over the loss of a six-week-old embryo is usually only a trifle as great as the grief occasioned by the loss of a ten-year-old child. We regard this as normal. Why should we not?

What people do is a better guide to how they feel than

what they say. What they say is too much affected by fashion; by hypocrisy; by cant.

By their actions people show that no one really believes in the equal value of all stages of human existence. Biology backs them up. Ethical theory must accommodate to what is simultaneously the intuitive insight of common people and the hardheaded conclusion of the most rigorous biological theory. If ethics and the law derived from it do not succeed in this we will be in deep political trouble.

16
YOU'VE MURDERED BEETHOVEN!

Oh, but that's only an analogy! After all, a house isn't a human being.

Quite. Analogy is not identity. All analogies ultimately fail. The question is: when an analogy fails, does the failure matter for the concern at hand?

Our concern is an ethical one.

When the blueprint analogy fails, is the failure ethically important?

The first failure is this: the blueprints of a house are *not* incorporated into the final structure itself, but the "blueprints" of a person are. Almost every one of the cells of the body—and there are 100,000,000,000,000 of them—has a complete set of blueprints in it. In this, a living body is remarkably different from a house.

But what ethical difference does it make? Are we constrained to cherish blueprints? Every time you brush your teeth you destroy hundreds of gum cells, each with a complete set of human blueprints. *So what?*

On the other hand, suppose the blueprints of a house

were to be found in every brick and stick—would it matter? Would the working blueprints thereby be made more valuable?

So, interesting though this failure of the analogy may be, it has no ethical significance.

Two physicians are talking shop. "Doctor," says one, "I'd like your professional opinion. The question is, should the pregnancy have been terminated or not? The father was syphilitic. The mother was tuberculous. They already had four children: the first was blind, the second died, the third was deaf and dumb, and the fourth was tuberculous. The woman was pregnant for the fifth time. As the attending physician, what would you have done?"

"I would have terminated the pregnancy."

"Then you would have murdered Beethoven!"

To anyone who loves music the story has a terrific impact. Despite all one's love of justice one is tempted to say that one Beethoven justifies the sacrifice of millions of unwillingly pregnant women.

But before we go off the deep end, let's try out a variation on the theme:

Two physicians are talking shop. "Doctor," says one, "I'd like your professional opinion. The question is, should the pregnancy be terminated or not? The paternal ancestors were a wandering, vagabond lot. They stuck neither to their jobs nor to their sexual partners. The man we are faced with is like his forebears. He was conceived out of wedlock, and his father didn't bother to legitimize him until he, the son, was thirty-nine years old. His first marriage was sterile. His second was a shotgun marriage. His third marriage was to a cousin, for which incestuous union he had to get a Bishop's dispensation. The first child of this marriage died in infancy. So did the second child. Now his wife is pregnant for the third time. What would you recommend?"

"This world is so crowded that I don't think any child should be born unless all the major indicators, both genetic and social, are favorable. I would recommend that this embryo be aborted."

"Then you would have murdered Hitler!"

Four bridge hands have been dealt out and are lying face down on the table. Before anyone can pick up his hand a cry of "Fire!" is heard and everyone rushes out of the house, which burns to the ground.

When it is all over the fire chief turns to two men who are weeping.

"Which of you is the owner?" he asks.

"I am," says one.

The fireman looks in puzzlement at the other. "And what are *you* crying about?" he asks.

"I didn't get a chance to look at my hand. I feel sure it must have been a hand of thirteen spades!"

What if your mother had aborted you?

How often have I been asked this question! There is no answer, of course. But there is a suitable reply:

Maybe she did.

The I who was aborted can't hear the question, and is beyond caring. The I who hears the question can make no sense of it, and cares not.

When the blueprints for a house are destroyed we can get another set that is an exact duplicate.

But when an embryo is destroyed, we will never see its like again.

Never? For all practical purposes, never. The genetic cards shuffled in the hereditary process are far more numerous than the fifty-two playing cards in a deck. The probability for any particular hand of cards in bridge—say thirteen spades—is about one in 635,013,559,600. The probability that the particular genetic blueprint of an aborted embryo will be exactly duplicated in a subsequent conception is much less than that.

So what?

What is lost, on the average, is the average. Neither Beethoven nor Hitler. Just average.

Probably.

As far as we will ever know.

Of the nonexistent nothing useful can be said.

Perhaps we should ask this question: Why should anyone seek meaning in the nonexistent? Is such seeking a cry for more life, by one who feels he has not had enough? What is it that is really bothering him?

With Spinoza I hold that "a free man thinks of nothing less than of death." Unfortunately there are too few free men and women in this world. By diminishing the number of unwanted children born we should be able to increase somewhat the proportion of free souls.

17
THE EARLIER THE BETTER

Set the speed limit at 60, and some motorists will drive 65.

THE EARLIER THE BETTER

Set the limit at 65, and some will drive 70.

Set it at 70, and some will go 80 . . . and so on.

Such is a common defect of arbitrary limits: *people push at the limit.*

This is not a problem with abortion. Set the limit at twenty weeks, and women will not seek to delay until a later time. Quite the contrary. A woman who wants an abortion wants it early. *The earlier the better.* She knows that if she delays until quickening, her psychology may change. The psychic pain will likely be greater. She knows also that the later the abortion, the greater the danger. And the greater the physical pain.

Late abortions are caused by officious committees making women wait in line for abortion—as they did in Sweden after 1939. When abortions are instantly available, as they have been in Hungary for twenty years, almost all the abortions are very early.

In the 1950s the maternal death rate from abortions was fifty times as high in Sweden as it was in Hungary. There was nothing wrong with Sweden's hospitals. It was the abortion committees that were at fault.

The earlier the better, that's what women think. They don't push at the line. Almost all freely permitted abortions occur early. (Exceptions are discussed in the next chapter.)

What we really need is a morning-after pill, something that could be taken within a few days after intercourse, causing a painless abortion. Or perhaps a once-a-month pill, taken just before the expected beginning of menstruation, and causing abortion if any implantation of an embryo had taken place. Such a substance would psychologically be perceived as a *menstruation-regularizer*. The woman wouldn't know whether she had been momentarily pregnant or not. She would cease to think about abortion, though she might have a dozen "silent" abortions a year.

A number of substances that might have such an effect are now being investigated. Women may already be using unlabeled abortifacients. Some of the formulations of the pill may be as much abortifacient as contraceptive in their action.

The IUD may cause abortions.

Not much research is being done to settle the question of the mode of action of these presumed contraceptives because many researchers feel it doesn't matter. So long as we have a vigorous antiabortion lobby, ignorance may be better than knowledge.

But isn't contraception always preferable to abortion?
Not necessarily.

The full-strength pill has about a 1 percent failure rate, and produces some undesired side effects. Very occasionally it causes blood clots. A dilute pill, the mini-pill, has fewer side effects, but a failure rate of about 3 percent.

Which is better, fewer side effects or less-frequent abortions? This is a technical question for doctors to solve with particular patients in mind. There is no one right answer.

The preferred answer depends on a comparison of—

1. the state of the art of contraception with—
2. the state of the art of abortion.

We don't know what future technology holds in store.

We should keep our options open. What are technically abortions may ultimately be safer than other forms of birth control. If that day comes, outlawing abortions would be forcing women to accept a greater risk rather than a lesser. It would be hard to justify that in any society that puts great store by the rights of the individual.

Anticipating such a technological advance we would be unwise to make any categorical condemnation of abortion now.

18
CRUEL LOGIC

There is one case in which the rule "the earlier the better" cannot be followed: the case of the deformed embryo.

Actually, the most seriously deformed embryos are spontaneously aborted in the first few weeks. We know this from examining spontaneous abortuses. These present no moral problem. That which some parents would not have the courage to do, Nature does for them.

Problems arise when a defective embryo is *not* spontaneously aborted, and the parents learn that it is defective (or that there is a high probability that it is). Unfortunately, this knowledge is often not gained until the pregnancy is advanced to 20 to 24 weeks. Quickening has already occurred, and may have left a psychological imprint on the mother. The time is late.

Detection is the problem. If a defect is suspected, the doctor can thrust a sterile hypodermic needle through the mother's abdominal wall, through the uterine wall and the placenta, through the embryonic membranes, and into the fluid-filled sac around the embryo. From this he can withdraw fluid and floating cells. The technique is called amniocentesis.

The physician's problem is to thrust the needle into the amniotic sac but not into the embryo. There are a number of precautions he can take, but in the end there is a small chance that he will damage the embryo. So it is not recommended that amniocentesis be made a routine procedure. There aren't enough capable doctors in the country to examine nearly four million embryos a year without producing more defects than would be detected.

Amniocentesis should be done only by specialists and only if there is strong reason to suspect a deformity. The fluid that is drawn off can be examined chemically. The floating cells can be cultured and examined both chemically and microscopically.

Then the doctor may recommend abortion. (Presumably the woman is willing to consider abortion, otherwise there would be little point in submitting herself to amniocentesis.)

As concerns abortion, the rule is, *the earlier the better*. But for amniocentesis, *the later the better*. When the embryo is tiny it is hard to thrust the needle into the mother without damaging the embryo.

A compromise is called for. In practice, amniocentesis is usually delayed until the 18th or 20th week. If cells must be cultured before they can be examined, it may be the 24th week before the mother gets the bad news.

This is very late. It's hard on the mother. But that's the way it is. (We can only hope that future technological developments will make the experience less harrowing.)

There certainly is no danger of "escalation," of mothers pushing for later and later abortions. It is only technological limitations that push the date as late as it is.

Nor is there any danger of the numbers increasing very much. Only 1 to 4 percent of all babies born are congenitally defective. (What percentage depends on what the standards are for defective.) In only a fraction of these cases is the suspicion of a defect strong enough to justify amniocentesis. Only some kinds of defects can be so detected.

All told, it is doubtful if the percentage of cases calling for amniocentesis will ever rise above 1 percent of all births. There is no need to view this as the thin edge of any important moral wedge.

Congenital deformity is only a minor reason for induced abortion. Yet the need in this minor class has been accepted as a justification of abortion more than any other, except for the still rarer class "to save the life of the mother." In the early 1960s opinion polls showed that 80 to 90 percent of the people approved of elective abortion if the embryo was known to be defective. At the same time, only about 10 percent approved of abortion on the simple request of the woman.

As we have learned, the percentage of the latter has risen to 64 percent. The former group is now in the high 90s. Almost everyone approves of aborting a defective embryo. Yet the Right-to-Lifers recognize no moral difference between abortion of a perfect embryo and abortion of a grossly deformed one. Not only do they say (quoting the words of the children's author "Dr. Seuss"), "A person's a person no matter how small."

They also imply: "An embryo's a person no matter how gruesome."

Their position is in total opposition to that of the rest of the population. *So they keep very quiet about this.*

But such is their position. The Twenty-eighth Amendment, if it comes into being, will remove the freedom that almost every woman wants to have, the freedom to spare defective embryos the defective lives they would have if they were allowed to continue with development.

The logic of Right to Life allows no escape from this cruel consequence.

19
THE ULTIMATE RIGHT?

No position is so ridiculous that someone cannot go it one better.

Beyond Right to Life lies SOUL—Save Our Unborn Lives. This group's motto (which they are said to have made into a bumper sticker, though I haven't seen it) is: *Every Child Has the Right to Be Conceived.*

Right-to-Lifers maintain that every fertilized egg has a right to be born. SOULs go even further, maintaining that every egg or sperm cell has a right to fulfill its destiny and unite with a reproductive cell of the opposite sex. The fertilized egg then has the right to be born.

Their position is not without its difficulties.

Given that the number of adult men is approximately equal to the number of adult women, for every egg cell produced about 31 billion sperm cells are produced.

SOUL to the contrary notwithstanding, there have to be a lot of "unsatisfied" sperm cells.

Will SOUL settle for having every egg cell fertilized (and let most of the sperm cells go down the drain)? How many egg cells does a woman produce?

Surprising as it seems, a clearcut answer to this simple question is not possible at this time. The ovaries seem to produce between 10,000 and 100,000 cells that are potential egg cells. But, of course, most of these do not normally become actual, fully functional eggs. Releasing one egg a month—usually—for thirteen lunar months each year between the ages of fifteen and forty-four, a woman produces a total of 390 fertilizable eggs.

Does SOUL expect women to produce 390 offspring each? Only with Brave New World-type artificial uteruses would this be possible.

Perhaps SOUL merely expects each woman to bear 30 children, one each year for 30 years?

This is a more modest demand.

But perhaps the women should be consulted.

As one might predict, SOULs have no sympathy with the "population nuts." In one of their newsletters the editor writes:

> What with all the talk about population control, the unconceived have little chance to be heard. Because they cannot speak for themselves, we try to speak for them. No so-called "civil liberty" should allow humans *already* born to snuff out the lives of the unconceived. Every child has the right to be conceived. . . .

Congress just passed a bill which would appropriate millions of dollars to a "crash program" of family planning. "Family planning" is an innocent phrase, but we know what it *means!* Let's get some telegrams in to our Senators and Representatives. If we let them successfully silence one segment of humanity, WHO WILL BE NEXT?

Who indeed?

20
YOU CAN'T PHOTOGRAPH MORALITY

The lights have been dimmed in the service club, and a picture flashes on the screen. It is a grotesque little embryo, in real life no larger than one's thumb, but now blown up six feet tall on the screen. It is in color, of course. How else can one show BLOOD?

Thus the Right-to-Lifers once more use their most effective weapon—color slides of embryos. The photography is excellent, the color garishly dramatic. Most people have never seen real embryos. *Life* magazine published some fine photos once, but now *Life* is dead. Memory fades. Novelty can shock, and Right-to-Lifers take advantage of this.

That audiences are shocked by Right-to-Life shows, and often shocked into suspending their reasoning processes, is a disparaging reflection on biologists as educators. If we biologists had made Johnny and Suzy Citizen, while they were pupils in the public schools, thoroughly familiar with embryology—both in its intellectual and its visual aspects—they would not now be shocked by color photos of embryos. But biologist-educators failed, and now everyone is paying the price.

The emotional effectiveness of photographs of embryos is rooted in ambivalence. The embryos both resemble, and do not resemble, adult human beings.

See!—there are five tiny fingers on each hand. In higher magnification you can see the wee fingernails. How precious!

Thus people "identify" with the tiny embryo, accepting it as a human being. At the same time, the whole embryo is grotesque. In its proportions it looks far less human than an adult monkey does. The grotesqueness arouses feelings of pity.

Viewing the slides we feel both attracted and repelled by the human-nonhuman ambivalence. A good Right-to-Life lecturer—and some of them are very good—capitalizes on this ambivalence.

Thought-experiment: Suppose the six-foot-tall projected picture of a twenty-four-week-old embryo came to life, stepped down off the screen, and walked toward you: What would you do?

You probably would run screaming from the room. At that size the creature would look less like a human being than it would like the Man from Mars constructed for a horror movie.

Of course, by further development, an embryo can become something everyone recognizes as human. That is the wonderful thing about biology. But the embryo itself would not really be acceptable as human.

Potential, remember, is not actual.

It is significant that the embryos most used by the Right-to-Lifers in their shows are late embryos—20 weeks and older.

But only a minority of abortions occur at so late a stage. If women had their way, the number would be zero. The factors that keep the minority above zero are three:

1. Technological limitations (difficulty of early amniocentesis, which is needed for detection of defects)
2. Administrative roadblocks (created by the pressure of those of the Right-to-Life persuasion)
3. Special cases (human behavior is so variable we can never foresee and plan for all the situations that turn up)

The trend in abortion is steadily toward the early stages. Most abortions now are performed on embryos so imperfectly formed that only the specialist can recognize them as embryos of human beings. Photos of these early embryos don't have the visual impact the Right-to-Lifers want, so they don't often show them. Yet—according to Right-to-Lifers—the moral problem of aborting even the earliest embryo is the same as it is with the latest.

One other trick of the Right-to-Lifers needs exposure. Their shows feature a great abundance of mangled embryos and fragments of embryos, all in glorious and repulsive color. The inference they want the viewer to make is that he is seeing the innocent victim of a crime —the crime of abortion, the crime of murder.

But you can't photograph morality: the picture of the

result of an act doesn't prove its cause. Looking at a photograph of the most thoroughly mangled embryo we realize that the explanation may be completely innocent (even by Right-to-Lifers' standards).

Here's an instance. A woman begins to abort spontaneously, but the process fails to complete itself. The embryo is dead but not expelled. The woman is taken to the hospital and a physician completes the abortion with surgical tools that mangle the embryo—which is then in fine condition for a Right-to-Life slide show.

The camera cannot reveal the innocent origin of the mangled embryo. Nor prove an evil origin, either.

Only the end result is captured by the camera—but that's all that Right-to-Lifers want.

There is a more fundamental criticism of the photographic approach to ethical problems: it focuses—note the verb—on things rather than systems.

Recall the story of Margaret in chapter 6. If you wanted to present her problem fairly *in pictures*, what would you photograph? Bloody embryos? Certainly not. Right-to-Lifers would, of course. Then what would be your photographic response? A picture of Margaret? Of her husband? Of the other woman? Of her children? Of her place of work? None of these will do individually, and all of them together are not much better. A "photo essay" may do the job, but only if the essay—an arrangement of words—is well written.

A skillful movie—a documentary or a screenplay with professional actors—might suffice. But think of the time and expense required to produce a movie in comparison with the time and expense required to produce a slide show of mangled embryos.

Still photos are admirably suited to showing pictures of *things*. At the very least, it takes movies to show pictures of *systems*. Moral problems are always embedded in systems of people and relationships. Movies are the least that will suffice, but even these are better augmented with words. And all of these together are not enough unless one mind makes contact with another, unless the speaker convinces the listener of the complexity of moral problems. When morality is to be understood, the camera alone is counterproductive.

The crowding of the world and the dizzy pace of technological change create an ever greater amount of information to be dealt with by the citizenry. *Information-overload*, it has been called. Photography has been hailed as a sovereign remedy for information-overload.

Faced with the emotionally effective photo shows of the Right-to-Lifers the opponent of mandatory motherhood is tempted to use equally gory photographs of women who have died of septic abortions, self-induced or carried out by amateurs. Such photos exist. They *are* gory. But I think it is a moral mistake to use them, just as it is for the Right-to-Lifers to use mangled embryo photos. Both propaganda approaches obscure the ethical issues.

In straightforward, noncontroversial matters photography may help. But in controversial matters it hinders. The camera is beautifully suited for biased presentations. (Even the placing of the tripod requires choosing a biased view at the outset.) The resulting biased picture unleashes a torrent of objections by those of other persuasions. In the end, the volume of words is increased rather than decreased by the introduction of the camera.

The Chinese say that one picture is worth a thousand words. But it may take ten thousand words to validate it.

21
WHAT IS INFORMED CONSENT?

In 1973, following the Supreme Court decisions, Right-to-Lifers threw a diabolically clever bill into the legislative hoppers of a number of states. What they proposed was just this: that no woman be allowed the abortion she requested until she had sat through a sufficiently long movie of abortions being performed on other women.

In color, of course.

The proposal is fiendishly clever because it exploits some of our best ideals. All the "best people" nowadays are in favor of freedom of information. The more information the better. And *informed* consent—is that not always to be preferred to uninformed consent? How can anyone who is so liberal as to be in favor of abortion be so illiberal as to be against informed consent?

So runs the argument. And it *is* plausible.

But only superficially so. A simple thought-experiment reveals the error. Suppose a state legislature enacted the following law:

> Section 47.3. No person shall be allowed to have his or her tonsils surgically removed until he/she has placed on file with the district attorney a signed and witnessed statement that he/she has viewed a ten-minute color film of tonsillectomies. Any explanatory commentary accompanying the film must be made equally by two commentators, one of

whom shall be a member of either the Church of Christ Scientist or Jehovah's Witnesses. If the person seeking the tonsillectomy is a minor, such of his/her parents as may still be alive must also witness the film and sign the statement filed with the district attorney.

Would we tolerate such a law? Or a similar one applying to any other operation? Only abortion is seen (by some) as so special that it needs to be hemmed in by law.

It is surely a reasonable guess that *some* people would back out of *any* operation, no matter how badly it was needed, if they first had to look at a color movie of it. So is informed consent always better than uninformed?

The following table resolves the difficulty.

Dependence of Consent on Information

State of Information	Consent Given?
1. Very little experience and information	Yes
2. Some experience and information	No
3. A great deal of experience and information	Yes

As concerns the medical treatment of himself, a physician is in situation 3. He has a great deal of experience and information, and has long since grown past the point where blood and scalpels scare him. If intellectual analysis convinces him that he needs to be operated on, the physician gives his consent, no matter how bloody the prospects.

On the other hand, the layman—the person with

almost no exposure to the sight of operations—consents to an operation either for purely intellectual reasons (his physician having adequately informed him) or simply because he has faith in his physician. He is in situation 1.

The most unhappy situation is that of the layman who has been given a *little* information in the form of color movies, just at the time when his anxiety is greatest (situation 2). We should not be surprised when such a person says no. He is informed, but not informed enough; experienced, but not experienced enough.

In economic and practical terms, it is easy and cheap to give enough information to cause a person to say no to a needed but bloody operation. It is inexpensive of both time and money to move a person from situation 1 to situation 2.

It is much harder and more expensive to give him or her the wealth of experience needed to produce a thoroughly informed consent, that is, to move him all the way to situation 3.

Right-to-Lifers, always considerate of the well-being of taxpayers, do not (of course) propose saddling taxpayers with the expense of producing a *thoroughly* informed public.

22
PREMATURE SIMPLIFICATION

It's hard to keep the "thin edge of the wedge" from entering a controversy over the value of life. The Hogan Amendment, offered in 1973, said: "Neither the United States nor any State shall deprive any human being of life on account of illness, age, or incapacity."

First, fetuses; next, the senile; *and next—ME!*

This, I think, is the train of thought many Right-to-Lifers are caught in. The psychological association is, I think, ethically unproductive. Abortion and euthanasia are such different problems that they can hardly be treated in a single formula.

"Ah!" says the Right-to-Lifer, *"You're afraid.* You know that abortion is only the entering edge of the wedge. You seek to hide the rest of the wedge from your audience. You are not completely candid."

It would be nice if I could point out that support of abortion and belief in the desirability of euthanasia are utterly independent of one another. If opponents and supporters of abortion were equally likely to support euthanasia my position would be easier to defend.

But I am afraid this is not so. I know of no opinion polls on the subject, but I would give heavy odds that abortion supporters are more inclined than people in general to support euthanasia.

"How do you explain that?"

The Right-to-Lifer has a simple answer: "People who deny the sanctity of life in one situation cannot support it in any situation whatever. Kill inch-long embryos today, and tomorrow you will have no compunction about killing your aged mother, once her existence has become inconvenient to you. By insensible but inevitable steps, abortion leads to Buchenwald." *

---

* Embarrassingly, for the Right-to-Lifers, the historical sequence in Germany ran the other way. One of the first things the Nazis did on coming into power in 1933 was to completely outlaw abortion, making it a capital offense for both the woman and her abortionist. Buchenwald came sev-

PREMATURE SIMPLIFICATION

The opponent of mandatory motherhood is likely to say something like this: "Support for abortion and support for limited, carefully regulated euthanasia are associated because both are associated with rationalism. Once you've begun to think you can't stop—and traditions tumble."

There's no easy reconciliation of the two positions.

I think there is little doubt that some of those who oppose abortion do so because they are afraid that denying the sanctity of life for fetuses will deny it for them next.

Curious: I *support* abortion for exactly the same reason.

As one about to enter the seventh decade of his life I am filled with horror at the thought that I may not be able to quit this life when the quality of it, as I see it, has sunk to so low a level that life is more a burden than a blessing.

Or, my mind may go first and I may then be incapable of reaching a decision. Contemplating such a time now, I hope someone puts an end to my life then. (It is no use asking how I will feel then.)

"But what if someone uses a permissive law to put you away before such a time—to settle an old grudge, perhaps, or to inherit your estate?"

Well, my estate is not enough to tempt anyone; but I have accumulated my proper share of enemies. So, it could happen. But I don't lose any sleep over it. To have enemies is the normal condition in life. The realist learns

---

eral years later, and the Nazis never relaxed the punishment against abortion. So where's the wedge?

to be happy in the midst of them. And if one of my enemies slips through the defenses, misericord in hand, and . . .

I have said before, and I still believe, that there is little psychological difference between the contemplation of sleep and the contemplation of death. "We die, and come to life, three hundred and sixty-five times a year. Finally there comes the year in which we come to life again only three hundred and sixty-four times." *

Pascal wrote: "There is nothing more real than death, nor more terrible."

To me, there is nothing more false than this statement of Pascal's.

Who's right, him or me? Undoubtedly, that's a bad question. We are different. There is probably no possibility of bringing two such minds into agreement.

The political problem is one of coexistence. Let those who fear death reject abortion and all forms of euthanasia—*for themselves and possibly for the loved ones they control.*

Let those who do not fear death act otherwise *in their own lives.*

The Right-to-Lifers' attempt to find a single verbal formula—"the sanctity of life"—to solve all problems of human existence is understandable. I would use such a simple approach myself, if I thought it would work.

But is the death of an embryo no different from the death of a comatose elderly patient, merely because the

---

* Garrett Hardin, *Exploring New Ethics for Survival: The Voyage of the Spaceship Beagle* (New York: Viking, 1972), p. 231.

single word "death" is applied to both? The psychological consequences for other members of society are completely different.

With an embryo, it's *all promise and no memories*.

With the senile, it's *all memories and no promise*.

Someday, we should be able to find a course of action with respect to the senile that will be acceptable to all non-Pascalians. For the present, I think we are clear only on abortion.

To a scientist, the problem is one of guarding against premature simplicity in analysis. A historical example may help illustrate the point.

In ancient times the Greeks thought the world was made of only four kinds of elements: earth, air, water, and fire. The analysis helped a little bit in understanding the world, but not much. It was too simple. By the nineteenth century molecules and atoms had been distinguished, and presently chemists agreed that there were ninety-two different kinds of atoms (elements). Then isotopes were found, and the number of elements rose to over a hundred, or to several hundred (depending on how you interpret the word *element*).

Too many. Deeper simplicity was sought, and thirty-two "fundamental particles"—electron, proton, meson, and the like—were distinguished. And tomorrow? Perhaps tomorrow still more fundamental units may be uncovered and the number reduced to four. Or two. Or perhaps even one.

But if the number is reduced to four it won't prove that the Greeks were right after all. In the deepest operational sense it will be a different four.

The simplicity introduced by the Greeks was a premature simplicity. For chemistry to develop, a less simple scheme was necessary. At each stage in the growth of science, experience dictates the appropriate simplification. "To the solid ground of Nature trusts the mind that builds for Age," said Wordsworth—and there are no Nobel prizes for premature simplifiers.

The "sanctity of life" is surely a premature simplification. The intention is praiseworthy, but as an analytic conception it just won't do.

23
HOW A MINORITY CAN TAKE OVER

Everyone has heard that "eternal vigilance is the price of liberty," and knows that democracy may be overthrown and replaced by a dictatorship. What is not so widely known is that even in a continuing democracy laws can be changed undemocratically. This is not, perhaps, a common occurrence, but it does happen.

It might happen with abortion.

The majority of the people are in favor of abortion-on-request. This was shown by the Gallup Poll in 1972 (see Appendix B). A total of 64 percent said yes to the question, "Do you agree that the decision to have an abortion should be made solely by a woman and her physician?"

Sixty-four percent is certainly a majority.

But the minority may yet have its way. Here's how it could happen.

A minority probably won in 1919 when the Prohibition Amendment was passed. (There was nothing like a Gallup Poll in those days, so we don't know for sure.)

HOW A MINORITY CAN TAKE OVER

Laws governing sexual behavior, obscenity, and the like are notorious for reflecting minority views.

But how can a minority win in a democracy? It sounds impossible.

In a simon-pure democracy a minority cannot win. Since everybody votes on every issue the majority always wins. No problem.

But only a very small community can afford the luxury of pure democracy. A few hundred is the limit; or perhaps a few thousand. After that, "Town Hall" has too many voices, too much talk. Time, always limited, runs out. So pure democracy must give way to representative democracy.

On the average, every 500 thousand Americans are represented by one Congressman, and every 4 million by two Senators. In various ways, our representatives "listen" to us. Can they always detect a majority opinion? Or if they can, are they always governed by it?

Money talks, of course—and sometimes louder than voters. But money is not always significantly involved. There is no reason to think that it is crucially important in the abortion issue. (Physicians do not write to their congressmen urging abortion so they can make more money in surgery. Such small pressure as there has been from the medical profession has mostly been from the other direction.)

If you want to stay in politics your first problem is to get reelected. From the way elected representatives behave, it is obvious that loud voices among their constituents have more effect than soft ones. The final "reading" of public sentiment is not determined merely by the number of voices on each side. Rather, the pressure from each side is the product of the number of voices multiplied by the emotional intensity expressed in those voices.

A more exact analysis can be made. A minority usually feels more strongly about an issue than the majority. Either openly or by hints, the minority says this to its representative: Whether or not I vote for you in the next election will be determined by your vote *on this issue alone*.

If 30 percent of a representative's constituency adopts the minority viewpoint he stands to lose 30 percent of his support if his vote is "wrong" (as the minority sees it).

The majority, on the other hand, is usually more confident and more nearly interested in a number of issues. Members of this group typically consider the *total* voting record of their representatives in deciding whether to support him in the next election. If there are ten significant issues, perhaps only a tenth of a congressman's majority support will desert him, if he votes "wrong" on one (as the majority sees it). Ten percent of 70 is 7. (The numbers are not precise, but they reveal the logic of the situation.)

Given a 70-to-30 split among the public, by voting *against the minority*, a representative loses *30 percent* of his support. By voting *against the majority*, he may lose only 7 percent.

It takes only a very few emotional issues like this to make a representative lose the next election if he votes with the majority on every issue. Knowing this, he may vote with a minority.

HOW A MINORITY CAN TAKE OVER

Thus can a minority prevail in a representative democracy.

Thus may a Right-to-Life Amendment become the law of the land, even though most of our citizens are against mandatory motherhood.

One further point about the dynamics of minority action needs to be pointed out.

Accompanying the Civil Rights movement of the last twenty years there has been a growing sympathy with minority interests. The majority is often fully aware that the minority is using the machinery of representative democracy to establish minority rule, as it were. But it does not object because it feels that it is only fair that the minority should obtain its *rights*, even if it can do so only by putting minority pressure on the representatives.

To put the matter another way: the majority recognizes that it is unfair for a majority to vote away a minority's rights.

But that is not what is involved in the abortion issue.

No one is denying the people in the minority the right to refuse abortions *for themselves*.

On the contrary, the minority is trying to deprive the majority of its freedom to have abortions.

It is sad when a majority deprives a minority of its freedom. It is even sadder when a majority passively allows its freedom to be destroyed by a militant minority. That hardly falls under the heading of intelligence or fair play.

24
A CASCADE OF CONSEQUENCES

Let's suppose that the majority has lost. The Twenty-eighth Amendment has passed both houses, has been signed by the President, and has been ratified by thirty-eight states.

The Right-to-Life Amendment.

The Mandatory-Motherhood Amendment.

What will life be like under the new law? This is a problem in legal assessment, which is every bit as difficult as technology assessment. No man is wise enough to lay out all the consequences of either technological or legal innovations; but the more crowded the world becomes the more important it is that we try to foresee both the major effects and the so-called side effects of an innovation of either sort before we adopt it.

The major effect of a Right-to-Life Amendment would be the legalization of mandatory motherhood. The side effects can be divided into two categories:

1. Effects under the law.
2. Effects outside the law.

Let's take up the legal side effects first.

I list only some of the more important side effects that occur to me. The reader can easily enlarge the list. There may well be some obvious effects that are more important than any I have thought of.

1. Demographic statistics will be altered, with chaotic results. All known spontaneous abortions must be registered as both births and deaths, making comparisons between pre- and post-Amendment days difficult. (This will be the least of our troubles.)

2. Since an aborted embryo is a dead human being, all legal burial requirements apply to it. Parents will be out an additional $300 to $1,000 for even a modest burial.

3. Because of the fear of "murder," research into the mechanism of action of contraceptives will be intensified. Right-to-Life organizations will push the federal government into funding such research on a generous scale.

4. No doubt some of the supposed contraceptives (e.g., the IUD) will be shown to be abortifacient in action. Those that are even a little bit abortifacient will be outlawed.

5. If a woman addicted to drugs has an unintended spontaneous abortion the district attorney may bring her into court on a charge of manslaughter. (Whether she is convicted or acquitted, who gains by this action?)

6. With the elimination of the backstop of abortion from the system of birth control, women will be unwilling to risk pregnancy by using gentle contraceptive medicines (which have a higher risk of failing to prevent pregnancy). Women will use the pill in the strongest formulations, thus increasing the frequency of its medically dangerous side effects.

7. Sometimes the best medical treatment for an ailing woman is one that probably, or certainly, will cause an abortion if she is pregnant. A doctor will not use such a treatment on a woman known to be pregnant, because he could be convicted of murder. The doctor will delay treatment until a pregnancy test has been carried out. If the treatment is prolonged, he will demand a pregnancy test every few weeks.

8. All this medical caution will result in poorer medical care for women (but not for men).

9. The poorer and more cautious medical care will increase the cost of caring for women. Because of the cost-sharing features of medical insurance, Medicare, et cetera, everyone will pay more, in premiums or taxes.

10. Since induced abortion will be legal murder, there will be more willingness than in the past to jail women who are convicted of having had criminal abortions. Jails, already crowded, will become even more so with the influx of women murderers. (Who gains by "progress" like this?)

11. There will be more employment for lawyers.

12. The dockets of courts will become longer still, and the delays of the law even more destructive of the sense of justice.

13. An embryo will have to be recognized as a dependent for income-tax purposes. (How does the Internal Revenue Service verify pregnancy?) Suppose a woman had three verified spontaneous abortions in a single year (which is perfectly possible). How many income-tax deductions does that give her?

Enough! Thirteen is a good enough number. You can take over from there. Think of the effects on automobile liability insurance. Think of the curious consequences in the legal area of wills.

Think . . .

Yes, that's right: THINK.

But: this won't be the first time we've had an abortion-prohibition law. Why didn't we have all those troubles before?

Simply for this reason: we were confused before. For

that much-extended Victorian century when abortion was forbidden, the crime of abortion was undefined.

It wasn't called murder.

It wasn't called manslaughter.

It wasn't identified as any familiar type of crime. It was just . . . abortion.

The Right-to-Lifers have now removed all ambiguity about this crime. It will be, if they have their way, *murder*. From this follow all the legal consequences listed above.

And more.

What about the illegal consequences? These were touched upon in chapter 3 where similarities of abortion-prohibition and alcohol-prohibition were pointed out. The list will bear repeating and adding to.

Bootlegging of abortion operations
Corruption of police
Corruption of the courts
Public disrespect of the law
Creation of an economic base for a Mafia
Encouragement of cynicism about the law among the young

Need we go on? Must we explicitly point out that the outlawing of contraceptives with abortifacient effects will result in the bootlegging of these drugs? And that bootlegged drugs inevitably become adulterated?

Must it be pointed out that defining so minor an act as an early abortion as an act of murder inevitably degrades the language? With the word *murder* used widely and loosely, our repugnance of the act of true murder—

by everyone's definition—will become diluted. This will remove some of the psychological deterrence of true murder.

The legal consequences of a Right-to-Life Amendment are comparatively easy to predict, for the law has an inner logic that is fairly well understood.

By comparison, the illegal consequences of such a law are much more difficult to predict. This is the area of sociology. Lacking an understood inner logic, the social world outside the law constantly shifts from one quasi-equilibrium to another. The first evasion of the law evokes an appropriate legal response. This evokes a second response from the law, which produces another extralegal response. This evokes a third response from the law, which produces another extralegal response. This consequence brings forth yet another, which. . . .

Right-to-Lifers intend to do only one thing: outlaw abortion.

But *we can never do merely one thing.*

We may not intend the cascade of consequences that follow from an ill-conceived action; but we are, in a deep sense, responsible for all that happens. The pity of it is that, in the matter of prohibition, we have historical experience to guide us—if we will only pay attention to past failures as we plan for the future.

The philosopher Santayana said: "Those who will not learn from the past are doomed to repeat it."

25
PROSPECTS FOR A SANE SOCIETY

The goal of medicine is the creation of a sound mind in a sound body. It is one of the paradoxes of medical practice that the literature it produces is almost wholly devoted to descriptions of unsound minds in unsound bodies. (It is as though painters showed their devotion to beauty by painting nothing but ugly pictures. Perhaps some do?)

However, the reason for the medical preoccupation with pathology is obvious enough that it doesn't need explaining. But, every once in a while, we do have to remind ourselves of the true goal of medicine.

This book has been almost wholly devoted to describing the horrors of life under a Right-to-Life law, together with the manifold and almost wholly bad consequences of mandatory motherhood. Yet the implicit concern is always the benefits of voluntary motherhood. It is best that the implicit now be made more explicit.

Until very recently, for all the hundreds of thousands of years of humankind's existence on earth, purely voluntary motherhood has been impossible because birth control was imperfect.

Of course, celibacy was a perfect form of birth control, but this was a practice one recommended only to enemies and competitors, for the most part. Even more was this true for sterilization, which, until modern times, was produced only by castration.

Only after contraception and abortion were added to the methods of birth control did it become possible to dream of a world in which motherhood would be a matter of choice. To our certain knowledge this great advance was begun at least four thousand years ago. But, until lately, realists could hardly dream of a world in which births were always wanted. Contraception was unreliable and abortion dangerous.

Not until the late-nineteenth century was there a rapid increase in the evolution of satisfactory techniques of birth control. A few thoughtful men understood the significance of the new technology, but it was mostly women who saw the vision of a new world. This is not to be wondered at: women were the prisoners of motherhood.

Women saw more clearly than men because their eyes were sharpened by suffering. They could pierce beneath the thick covering of sham and hypocrisy better than comfortable, complacent men.

And what did they see, these women who glimpsed the potential of a new tomorrow? Three things, it seems to me.

First: Freedom for women. Not absolute freedom—nobody has that. But a freedom approaching that which men enjoy. In the United States we removed the last legal justification for compulsory servitude in 1862. Insofar as laws can, the Emancipation Proclamation did away with compulsory servitude tied to race. But compulsory servitude tied to sex remained. (For motherhood, however great its joys, is a form of servitude.)

Then, in 1973, the Supreme Court destroyed the legal basis for compulsory servitude tied to sex, when it decreed that any woman wanting an abortion could have one. A system of birth control is absolutely reliable only if abortion is part of the system—the backup measure when other means fail.

So suddenly did the Supreme Court's decision burst on the world—so without warning—so surprising was it even to the proponents of abortion-on-request, that it is small wonder that the decision exacerbated the backlash of the Right-to-Life group.

Future shock.

The human mind cannot easily accommodate itself to fundamental social change. We must give reluctant minds time to adjust while endeavoring to limit backlash. We must be patient—without abandoning our ideals.

Second: Freedom for children. In the nature of things, children cannot be as free as adults. The consequences of their being socially as free as natural limitations admit would, in fact, be unmitigated horror. There's too much truth in *The Lord of the Flies* to advocate so great a freedom.

But it is indefensible to subject children to all the enslavements of the past. From the very beginning of the birth-control movement the desirability of greater freedom for children was regarded as almost as important as the freedom of women. Margaret Sanger, in 1916, gave the same speech to more than a hundred audiences (this was in the days before radio and television), and it ended always with the same ringing declaration: *"The first right of every child is to be wanted, to be desired, to be planned with an intensity of love that gives it its title to being."*

Third: Freedom for society. Society, a collection of individuals, functions poorly if its components are sick. The key components in this connection are women and children. (Men, who cannot bear children and who seldom devote themselves to the upbringing of children as much as women do, must play third fiddle in the reproductive arena.) Society cannot be healthy if its components do not enjoy good health—particularly good psychological health.

In the triad of the family, the health of the woman is paramount. Her psychic health requires that she be free to avoid children if—and when—she feels she cannot take good care of them. Abortion, like other forms of birth control, is primarily used for spacing births. The embryo aborted this year can be replaced by another a few years later when the earlier-born children are older. Children benefit by birth spacing, however achieved.

A woman who is forced to bear a child she does not want may never know the joy of having a wanted child. In the limited space of a mother's spirit an unwanted child can preclude a wanted child's ever moving into a welcoming place. The child wants his mother to want him.

Abortion for the children's sake—this is paradoxical but true.

And society wants children to be wanted so they have a reasonable chance of growing up without twists. (If they grow up physically or psychologically twisted, society pays grievously for their unwantedness.)

The great psychoanalyst Erik Erikson, looking hopefully into the future, has foreseen a day when "There will exist a well-informed, well-considered, and yet fervent public conviction that the most deadly of all possible sins is the mutilation of a child's spirit; for such mutilation undercuts the life principle of trust."

Without sufficient mutual trust society flies apart and chaos takes over.

Look over the works of the great authors of the last

two thousand years. How much discussion do you find in them of the importance of the psychological health of women and children to the creation of a healthy society? Very little. But that is because most of the "great" philosophers, theologians, and political scientists have been men, living in a male-dominated culture.

What would be the consequences if the number of psychologically warped adults could be reduced to a tenth the present proportion by seeing to it that no mother ever was compelled to bear an unwanted child, and every child born was a wanted child?

We have no historic model of such a world. The mind boggles when it tries to take in the momentous consequences of producing only wanted children.

I think it is especially hard for men to grasp the magnitude of the problem and the possibilities. I can never forget how struck I was by what a middle-aged woman said to me at the conclusion of a lecture on abortion.

"I agree with you," she said, "but it seems to me that you've missed one of the most important points. I've had a pretty hard life, I suppose, but I've had one thing going for me that millions of people don't have. No matter how bad things may have been for me at any particular time, I have always been absolutely sure that my parents wanted me. It would be hard to exaggerate the strength that certain knowledge has given me."

What she said opened my third ear. Since then I have become acutely aware of how many people there are in the world who lack the certain knowledge that they were wanted when they were conceived. Worse, a minority—but still a not small number—know damned well that they weren't wanted. This is a heavy cross to bear. We should not wonder if many grow up humpbacked under such a psychic load.

Right-to-Lifers see abortion as a purely negative thing, a killing, a murder, a loss of potential.

How wrong they are.

The unborn lives that are put to an end before the time for recognition as members of the community—which occurs at birth, in our society—by their disappearance contribute in a positive way to the psychological health of the surviving community.

Wherever there is mandatory motherhood, in every mind there must always be the gnawing doubt, *Was I really wanted?*

Only if tiny unwanted beings are removed before society confers on them the status of human beings (and thus right-full members of the human community) can all those who are born into the community be endowed with the psychic strength that comes from knowing for sure that they were wanted. Such knowledge must be nearly universal among its members if a society is to have a decent chance to become fully sane.

APPENDIXES

APPENDIX A

Organizations Supporting Abortion

The wide range of organizations supporting the repeal or substantial modification of abortion-prohibition laws is evident from the following list, which was compiled and published in 1972 by NARAL (see Appendix E). Right-to-Lifers try to give the impression that theirs is *the* religious position, so it is important to note the large number of religious organizations that oppose them.

American Association of Planned Parenthood Physicians
American Association of University Women
American Baptist Convention*
American Bar Association**
American Civil Liberties Union
American College of Obstetricians and Gynecologists
Americans for Democratic Action
American Ethical Union
American Friends Service Committee
American Home Economics Association
American Humanist Association
American Jewish Congress
American Medical Women's Association
American Protestant Hospital Association
American Psychiatric Association

* On request during first trimester.
** On request during first 20 weeks.

American Psychoanalytic Association
American Psychological Association
American Public Health Association
Association for Voluntary Sterilization
B'nai B'rith Women
Church Women United, Board of Managers
Citizens Advisory Council on the Status of Women
Clergy Consultation Service on Abortion
Episcopal Churchwomen of the U.S.A.
Federation of American Scientists
Fiftieth Anniversary Conference of the Women's Bureau of the U.S. Department of Labor
Group for the Advancement of Psychiatry
Izaak Walton League
Medical Committee for Human Rights
Moravian Church, Northern Province Synod
National Association for Repeal of Abortion Laws
National Association of Social Workers
National Committee for Children and Youth
National Conference of Commissioners on Uniform State Laws*
National Council of Jewish Women
National Council of Obstetrics-Gynecology
National Council of Women of the United States
National Council on Family Relations
National Emergency Civil Liberties Committee
National Medical Association
National Organization of Women
National Welfare Rights Organization

* On request during first 20 weeks.

National Women's Political Caucus
Physicians Forum
Planned Parenthood-World Population
Population Association of America
President's Task Force on the Mentally Handicapped
Sierra Club
Society for the Psychological Study of Social Issues
Student American Medical Association
Unitarian Universalist Association
Unitarian Universalist Women's Federation
United Automobile Workers Union
United Church of Canada, General Council
United Church of Christ
United Methodist Church
United Presbyterian Church in the U.S.A.
White House Conference on Children and Youth
Women's Division, United Methodist Church
Women's Liberation
Women's National Abortion Action Coalition
Young Women's Christian Association of the U.S.A.
Zero Population Growth, Inc.

APPENDIX B

Gallup Poll on Abortion

1

This Gallup Poll was taken in June 1972.
Question: "Do you agree that the decision to have an abortion should be made solely by a woman and her physician?"

	Agree %	Disagree %	No opinion %
TOTAL	64	31	5
Men	63	32	5
Women	64	31	5
Protestants	65	31	4
Catholics	56	39	5
Republicans	68	27	5
Democrats	59	36	5
Independents	67	28	5
College	74	22	4
High School	65	30	5
Grade School	47	45	8
East	69	27	4
Midwest	62	34	4
South	53	40	7
West	73	21	6
Less than $5,000	53	38	9
$5,000–$6,999	55	40	5
$7,000–$9,999	71	26	3
$10,000–$14,999	68	27	5
$15,000 and over	74	24	2
Under 30 years old	64	31	5
30–44 years old	63	33	4
45 and over	63	31	6

2

In March 1974 (more than a year after the Supreme Court decision) a Gallup Poll was taken on the following question: "The U.S. Supreme Court has ruled that a woman may go to a doctor to end pregnancy at any time during the first three months of pregnancy. Do you favor or oppose this ruling?"

The overall results:

Favor	47%
Oppose	44%
No opinion	9%

These results seem to be inconsistent with the ones obtained in the earlier poll. Has there been a reversal in sentiment?

Possibly. The Right-to-Life group may have succeeded in changing public opinion. But other interpretations are also possible. It is a well known fact of poll-taking that if you alter a question ever so slightly you get a different result. The wording of the question in March 1974 is quite different from that in June 1972. The earlier poll inquired into the appropriate behavior of a woman and her physician, deciding jointly. The later poll brought the Supreme Court into the act, implying a greater role for the woman with less power for the physician. These changes may well be significant. Many people are "down on" the Supreme Court for other reasons; and many others—male chauvinists of both sexes—do not trust women to make their own decisions. It is plausible that these facts account for the different results of the two polls. It would take another carefully run poll to see if what is plausible is in fact true.

APPENDIX C

The Swedish Study

Hans Forssman and Inga Thuwe, "One Hundred and Twenty Children Born After Application for Therapeutic Abortion Refused," *Acta Psychiatrica Scandinavica* 42 (1966): 71–88.

Introduction

The aim of the present study was to determine the mental health, social adjustment and educational level of children born after their mothers had applied for legal abortion on psychiatric grounds, and been refused. For this purpose we compared a series of children born of these pregnancies with an equally large control series, following all the subjects up to their 21st birthday.

Therapeutic abortion was first officially legalized in Sweden in 1939 and during the years of relevance to this study it was permissible on the following grounds (which are still valid):

When, because of disease, physical defect or weakness in the woman, the birth of the child would endanger her life or health.

When the pregnancy is the result of a felony, such as rape or incest, or intercourse with a girl under 15, or of the woman being made to submit to intercourse against her will because of being dependent on the man, or when it is any other way the result of gross violation of the woman's freedom of action.

When the expected child might inherit a mental disease, mental deficiency, or a severe physical disease or deformity, either from its mother or father.

On July 1, 1946, the law was broadened to include the following indication:

When, in view of the woman's living conditions or other circumstances, it can be assumed that the birth and care of the expected child will seriously undermine her mental or physical health.

This indication came too late for the mothers of the

present subjects. It has led to much debate in Sweden, but the psychiatrists at our hospitals seem to have based their recommendations for or against abortion on essentially the same grounds before 1946 as they did afterwards.

Much has been written about abortion during recent years. Among Swedish studies are: Lindberg's (1948) *What does the woman do when the psychiatrist says no to her application for abortion?*; the social worker Karin Malmfors' (1951) follow-up study of 200 women who had applied for abortion; Ekblad's follow-up study (1955) of 479 women granted an abortion on psychiatric indications; Arén and Åmark's (1957) study of the outcome in 244 cases of authorized but unperformed abortions; Arén's (1958) study of 100 newly delivered mothers who had a former pregnancy prematurely terminated on legal grounds; Kerstin Höök's (1963) follow-up study of 249 women refused a legal abortion. Schlaug (1952) studied the male partner in 488 cases of application for abortion. Ekblad's and Höök's publications also contained data on the men concerned.

Thus several studies have been made of the mothers and fathers involved in cases of abortion. But little has been written about the third member of the trio involved —the unwanted child. Arén and Åmark (1957) related that 12 out of 162 children born to women who had gone through with their pregnancy were sent to a foster home for permanent care or adoption. Malmfors (1951) related that 7 out of 85 children born after an application for abortion had been refused were left for adoption. These authors said nothing more about the fate of these children, and Arén and Åmark did not check their information in the official registers. Furthermore, both these studies were made between 3 and 5 years after the children were born, when they were too young to permit any conclusion about their mental health or social adjustment. Höök (1963) followed a number of features in 204 children in her series until they were 8½ years old, on the average, the ages ranging from 7 to 11½; 15 were left for adoption; the rest of her data about the children cannot be compared with any of the figures from the present study. This seems to be all that is written in Sweden about the fate of these unwanted children.

The Danish author F. B. Nielsen (1960), reported that, of 92 children born after application for abortion had been refused, 2 were stillborn, 82 healthy and 8 abnormal in some respect. But his children, too, were too young to permit any conclusion on their mental health and social adjustment.

It is beyond the scope of this investigation to go into the lengthy debate that has been going on about the legislation governing premature termination of pregnancy. Extensive reviews of this are given in the publications of Ekblad (1955) and Höök (1963).

The problem of abortion was given particular attention in the December 12, 1964, issue of the *Lancet*, which contained articles by Tredgold and by Uhrus and a leading article on the subject. The leading article concurred with the demand made at a meeting of U.S.A. specialists in 1955 for "more research into the background, motivation, mechanisms and results" of therapeutic termination of pregnancy.

As therapeutic abortion was not regularized by law in Sweden until January of 1939, it has hardly been possible until now to determine the long-term social and psychiatric consequences for the children born after application for abortion has been refused. In 1960 we published the preliminary results of this study in Swedish.

Material

Unwanted Children. The subjects studied came from Göteborg, Sweden's second largest city, with a population of about 280,000 at the time in question—1939–1942. During these years, the city had only one large general hospital, the Sahlgren Hospital. In October of 1938, a psychiatric department was opened at the hospital, and among its other activities, this department served as a counselling center for mothers seeking legal abortion. During the years of relevance to the present study, it was the only center of this kind in Göteborg. The few cases taken in hand by private practitioners during this period are not included in our series.

Thus, the material for this investigation originates from all the cases of women living in Göteborg who applied for a therapeutic abortion to the Psychiatric Department of the Sahlgren Hospital during the years 1939 to 1941, inclusive, and were refused. These included both the women coming only to the outpatient service and the ones hospitalized for observation. We took 1941 as the last year so that we could follow the children born of these pregnancies until the age of 21.

During the years 1939 to 1941, altogether 197 women

living in Göteborg had 199 applications for legal abortion refused, 2 women having been refused for two pregnancies. These do not include any woman who changed her mind and took back her application. In 188 of the 199, the psychiatrist at the department decided against abortion, in 10 cases, which had been referred to the Medical Board, the Board refused to authorize the abortion, and in one case, also referred to the Medical Board, the Board authorized the abortion but the obstetrician refused to do the operation because the pregnancy had proceeded too far.

Three of the 197 women could not be traced. One was a refugee who lived only a short time in Sweden. It is impossible to explain why the other 2 could not be traced; they may have given a false name or only a temporary address. This left 194 women and 196 refused applications.

Sixty-eight of these 196 pregnancies ended in abortion, spontaneous or provoked. Sixty-eight out of 196 is a large percentage—34.7 percent—and undoubtedly many of them were illegal. Since the drop-out rate is indicative to some extent of the kind of subjects chosen for study—the narrower the indications for legal abortion, the greater the number of illegal abortions—it is interesting to compare this figure with those from other Nordic countries on the frequency of interrupted pregnancy after legal permission for abortion had been refused. There is not much point in comparing our figures with those of other than these countries because the conditions differ too much.

Lindberg (1948) found that only 50 (14.5 percent)

did not give birth at the expected time out of all 344 women refused an authorized abortion after being admitted as inpatients to the Psychiatric Department of the Sahlgren Hospital between 1940 and 1946. Hultgren (1959) found that 14.4 percent of 4,274 women whose petitions for abortion had been turned down by the Medical Board during 1954 to 1956 did not go through with their pregnancy; 224 of the 4,274 were from Göteborg, and 35 of these 224 (15.6 percent) did not go through with their pregnancy.

Thus the percentage of prematurely terminated pregnancies, spontaneous or provoked, was smaller in these two Swedish series than in ours. It is true that all Lindberg's women had been under observation as inpatients, as against only 49 of our 199. One probably does not get such a good psychotherapeutic grip on patients only coming to an outpatient service as one does when they are hospitalized. On the other hand, only 83 of 136 Danish women refused legal abortion after observation at the Psychiatric Department at Frederiksberg's Hospital went through with their pregnancies, the drop-out rate in this series thus amounting to 39 percent (Delcomyn, 1952).

A more probable explanation for the difference is this. Lindberg's series comes from 1940–1946, Hultgren's from 1954–1956, and ours from 1939–1941. In 1939 the number of legally authorized abortions in Sweden amounted to 439, in 1946 it rose to 2,378 and in 1951 it reached a peak of 6,328; it then fell slightly, amounting to about 5,000 in 1952–1954, 4,562 in 1955, and 3,851 in 1956. Another way of following the trend is to compare the number of legal abortions with the number of livebirths during the same period. During 1939 to 1942, 0.5 pregnancies were terminated by legal abortion for every hundred livebirths. In 1946 the proportion rose to 1.8, and in 1951 to 5.7. In 1952 and 1954 it was 4.8, in 1955 it was 4.3, and in 1956 it was 3.6.

In short, many more authorized abortions were done after than during the years of relevance to our investigation. Because it was harder to get permission for therapeutic abortion in 1939–1941 than later it is reasonable to assume that more illegal abortions were performed in our series than in later series. Delcomyn (1952), comparing the Danish figures for 1945–1949 with those for 1950 and the first half of 1951, found that there were relatively more authorized abortions in the second period, and also that a larger percentage of the women refused a legal abortion went through with their pregnancy the second period. She gave no figures for her observation.

Thus 128 of the pregnancies in our series (representing 126 women) proceeded to term. The result was 134 children, including 6 pairs of twins. Four of the 134 were stillborn, and 8 died within a year, one before it was 2 and one before it was 3. Excluding these 14 cases of early death left 120 children. The present study is based on these 120 all of whom reached the age of 21. They include 4 pairs of twins and 2 twins whose partners had died. Table 1 shows the 120 divided by year of birth and sex.

Control Children. All but 1 of the 120 unwanted children were registered in Göteborg when they were born.

APPENDIX C

Table 1. The 120 children born after their mother's application for legal abortion was refused, by year of birth and sex

Year of birth	Boys	Girls	Total
1939	9	6	15
1940	32	13	45
1941	17	22	39
1942	8	13	21
Total	66	54	120

We chose control subjects for these 119 as follows: When the infant was born in one of the city's maternity hospitals, we took the next same-sexed child born in the same hospital for its control subject. For the 17 born elsewhere, we took the first same-sexed child registered in the city hospitals on the same day. When the control subject died before the age of 21, we replaced it with the first same-sexed child born after it in the same hospital. For control subjects for twins, we took the next pair of twins, same-sexed or bi-sexed as the case was, born in the same hospital. For the 2 children of twin birth, one of whose partners was stillborn and one died within 3 months, we chose control subjects as if the original children were singletons.

For the control subject of the child born outside Göteborg we took the next child of the same sex registered in the book of the same parish.

Sources of Data Analyzed *

* In these analyses we have called a p value of <0.05 probably significant, of <0.01 significant and of <0.001 highly significant.

From the civil and parish registry offices we found out: whether the would-not-be mother had had her child after her application was turned down; the addresses of the unwanted children and their control subjects from birth until they reached the age of 21; the marital status of the children and whether they in turn had had any children. One control subject lived in another country for six months when she was 18; apart from this we were able to follow every subject from the time they were born until they were 21.

From the child welfare boards (see p. 118) in the various districts in which the subjects had lived, we learned whether they had any of the subject's names in their files and, if so, why.

At the child-guidance clinics and youth psychiatry centers in the districts where the subjects lived or had lived we asked whether they had been consulted for mental deviation or illness in any of the subjects. We did the same at all the mental hospitals and psychiatric departments in general hospitals, and at all the psychiatric outpatient services in the districts where the subjects had lived after the age of 15. We also wrote to all the rural and urban psychiatric consulting bureaus run independently of the psychiatric departments in the general hospitals. We were not able to cover all the private practitioners who might have been consulted and we therefore disregarded anything we happened to hear from one of them having been consulted.

Sweden has a central penal register for the whole country, where every act of the authorities restricting the liberty of an individual is recorded, whether it be sentence to an adult or juvenile prison or internment in some other kind of an institution; also every instance of exemption from legal punishment because of legal irresponsibility, fines above a certain level and fines for crimes for which the alternative is penal servitude. All cases of conditional sentence are also recorded there. After receiving special permission from the government, we went through these files to see whether we could obtain any further evidence of antisocial conduct on the part of the subjects until they reached the age of 21.

We also inquired at all the official temperance boards and social agencies in the districts where the subjects lived after the age of 16. (Not until 16 are persons registered in their own names in the records of the social agencies.)

We inquired about the subjects' schooling in the various school districts to which they belonged. Whenever they proceeded to secondary schools, we inquired at these schools whether they had gone on from them to other forms of study, and about any examinations they had passed. Thus we have full information on all the examinations the subjects passed prior to university. We then learned whether they had studied at any university before the age of 21 by going through the annual lists of the students enrolled at the various Swedish universities.

The information we got from the schools and the files of the social agencies showed that there was no point in inquiring at the agencies for the education and care of the mentally retarded.

In Sweden military service is obligatory for men, but not for women. We inquired at the Swedish Institute of Military Psychology about the fitness group into which the male subjects had been classed, and, if they had completed their military service, about how they had succeeded with their duties there. As a rule the young men must enroll for military service the year they become 18, but they can put it off up to the age of 21 or more for reasons of health or education. When they did this, we sometimes extended our limit beyond the 21st birthday in this one respect.

Three subjects (1 original and 2 control subjects) were the children of leading citizens in small communities, and we felt that it would be unfair to make inquiries about them in the local agencies in their neighborhood. But we got all the information we needed about them from other sources and there being no difference between them and the other subjects in depth of penetration we have included them with the others in the various analyses.

Differences Between Original and Control Series

Age, Maternal Age and Social Group. The ages of the two series of subjects correspond almost to the day. The greatest difference amounted to 25 days (twin cases).

The unwanted children were born to mothers 30 years old on the average, the control children to mothers of 28, on the average. There is a significant difference here $(0.01 > p > 0.005)$.

We also compared the two series for the social group into which they were born, using the norms from the Swedish electoral statistics for the years 1937 to 1940. We did the grouping according to the father's occupation at the time, or if the mother was unmarried according to hers. Children adopted by couples neither of whom was their real parent, were grouped according to the occupation of the adoptive father at the time. But children adopted by men their mothers married after they were born were grouped according to their mothers' occupation when they were born. The result of this comparison is seen from table 2, which also shows how the inhabitants of Göteborg were distributed by social group in 1940.

Table 2. *The unwanted and control children, by original social group*

Social group	Number		Percentage		Whole of Göteborg in 1940
	Unwanted children	Control children	Unwanted children	Control children	
I	3	4	2.5	3.3	6.5
II	22	32	18.3	26.7	31.4
III	95	84	79.2	70.0	62.1
Total	120	120	100.0	100.0	100.0

More of the control than unwanted children were born into group II, and the reverse held for group III. Combining groups I and II gave 25 for the unwanted children and 36 for the control children, against 95 and 84 for group III. Thus the two series did not differ significantly in this respect ($p \simeq 0.10$), though no consideration was given to social group when choosing the control subjects.

Seventy-seven pairs, each consisting of one subject

from either series, belonged to the same social group; 43 did not.

Results of Comparing Family and Social Environment of Unwanted and Control Children

Insecure Childhood. We considered that the following circumstances in the history of the subjects pointed to an insecure childhood background:

1. Complaints to a child welfare board about the way the subjects were being treated at home.

Every local authority district in Sweden is required to set up a child welfare board whose duty is to see that all children in its district are properly cared for. Up until 1960 the boards were required to interfere whenever children under 16 were being exposed to physical or mental harm through cruelty or neglect at home, or in danger of becoming delinquent because of their parents' depravity, negligence, or inability to bring up their children.

2. The child taken into custody by a child welfare board for protective care.

If consulting with, advising or warning the parents had no effect, or if the board decided that it would be a waste of time to try to persuade the parents to mend their ways, the board had the right to take the child away from its parents for protective custody.

3. Placement in a foster home.

4. Placement in a children's home.

5. Childhood in broken home, i.e. loss of a parent through divorce or death before the child was 15, or birth out of wedlock not followed by legitimization.

Table 3 shows how many subjects in either series were brought up under each of these circumstances. As seen there, 32 (26.7 percent) of the unwanted children were born out of wedlock, against only 9 (7.5 percent) of the control children. The difference is highly significant ($p < 0.001$). Eighty-six pairs (one member from each series) agreed in regard to legitimacy; 34 did not. The parents legitimized 5 of the 32 unwanted children born out of wedlock by getting married 2 to 24 months after they were born, and the parents of 5 of the 9 illegitimately born control children did the same 2 to 33

Table 3. Comparison between unwanted and control children for circumstances in history pointing to insecurity in childhood (*The same child may occur in several categories*)

Circumstances pointing to insecure childhood	Unwanted children	Control children
Report to children's aid bureaus about unsatisfactory conditions at home	17	6
Child removed from home by authorities	2	0
Placement in foster home	19	4
Placement in children's home	30	10
Parents divorced before child was 15	23 ⎫	13 ⎫
Parent(s) died before child was 15	10 ⎬ 60	5 ⎬ 22
Born out of wedlock and never legitimized	27 ⎭	4 ⎭
Born out of wedlock and legitimized	5	5

months later. Eight of the unwanted children were adopted by others than their real parents (7 of these were illegitimate). None of the control subjects were adopted.

According to the criteria laid down, 72 (60 percent) of the unwanted children had an insecure childhood, as against only 34 (28.3 percent) of the control children. If one disregards the stays in children's homes, many of which were for only a short while, the figures change to 65 (54.2 percent) against 26 (21.7 percent), and the difference remains highly significant ($p < 0.001$).

In short, it is obvious that the children born after an application for abortion had been refused ran a greater risk of insecurity in childhood than did their control subjects.

Disposition to Move to Other Local Authority Districts. There being more delinquency in cities than in other regions we determined how many of either series had stayed the whole time in Göteborg. Another reason for doing so was that we had unusually good possibilities of getting complete information about these subjects since our place of work is in Göteborg. We also checked whether they differed in tendency to move from place to place.

Seventy-seven (62.2 percent) of the unwanted children stayed in Göteborg until they were 21, and 85 (70.8 percent) of the control subjects. Twenty-one (17.5 percent) of the unwanted children had lived in three or more local authority districts, and 19 (15.8 percent) of the control subjects. Thus the two series agreed well, both for permanency of residence in Göteborg, and for tendency to move from one district to another. There were 55 pairs in which both the original and control subject had lived the whole time in Göteborg.

Results of Comparing Personal Data in Original and Control Series

Psychiatric Consultation and Hospitalization. Thirty-four of the unwanted children (28.3 percent) had gone to a psychiatric clinic of some kind or received psychiatric care in a hospital. The corresponding figure for the control subjects was 18, or 15 percent. The difference is probably significant ($0.025 > p > 0.01$).

Twenty-nine of the unwanted children had been under the care of a child psychiatrist, 28 only as an outpatient, and one as an inpatient as well. Six had visited a center for adult psychiatry; 3 of these had been hospitalized, one in a psychiatric department at a general hospital, one at a mental hospital, and one at both. One of the latter belonged to the 29 who had gone to an outpatient department for child and youth psychiatry.

Fifteen of the control subjects had visited a center for child psychiatry, all of them only for outpatient treatment. Four had been patients at a center for adult psychiatry, 2 as an outpatient, one at a mental hospital, and one at both a mental department in a general hospital and a mental hospital. One of these 4 belonged to the 15 who had gone to a center for child psychiatry.

The question arises: Was it because the mothers of the unwanted subjects had been in contact with psychiatrists before the children were born that so many of these children were registered at centers for child psychiatry? It may be that, having once consulted a psychiatrist, these mothers found it easier to do so again, whereas the mothers of the control subjects, who had seldom if ever consulted a psychiatrist about themselves, did not go to a psychiatrist for their children unless something was seriously wrong. Likewise, the mothers who had consulted a psychiatrist about abortion might be more apt than others to seek psychiatric advice for other personal troubles afterwards, and if they then complained about their children being nervous, the child might very likely be sent to a psychiatrist while the perhaps equally nervous children of other mothers might not.

In 1959 we determined how many of the mothers up to that year had consulted a psychiatrist for matters not directly concerned with the abortion, but only among the mothers of the 57 pairs in which both partners had lived in Göteborg all the time up to then. Twenty-seven of the 57 would-not-be mothers had gone to one of the municipal psychiatric outpatient departments for complaints not directly concerned with the abortion, and 10 of their children had done so. The corresponding figures for the control series were 9 and 0. It is apparent from this that it was not because the would-not-be mothers had consulted a psychiatrist about abortion that these children went more often than the others to a child psychiatrist. When all the subjects reached the age of 21, the number of pairs living the whole time in Göteborg dropped to 55, but we did not consider it worth while to do the analysis again for this sake.

APPENDIX C

Delinquency and Crime. Our figures for acts of delinquent nature reported to the child welfare boards do not cover drunken misconduct; this will be taken up in the next section.

Twenty-two (18.3 percent) of the unwanted subjects, 19 boys and 3 girls, were registered with the child welfare boards for delinquency, against 10 (8.3 percent) of the control subjects, 9 boys and one girl. The difference is probably significant ($p < 0.05$).

The boards had made investigations in 12 of the first 22 subjects and in 4 of the second to determine whether formal charges brought against them should be dropped. This happened 19 times in the original series, 8 times in the control series. Three of the first series and one of the second were removed from their homes and placed in protective custody elsewhere, in accordance with the law then in force, according to which correctional measures must be undertaken when children under 18 show severe forms of maladjustment. One of these 3 unwanted children, as well as the control subject, was sent to a reformatory.

The penal register contained the names of 10 of the unwanted children (8.3 percent) and of 3 control subjects (2.5 percent). The difference is not significant ($0.10 > p > 0.05$). Nine of the first 10 were male, one was female. The control subjects were all male.

Drunken Misconduct. The records of the official temperance boards contained the names of 19 of the unwanted children (15.8 percent) and 13 control subjects (10.8 percent) for drunken misconduct. The difference is not significant ($0.50 > p > 0.30$). Two of the first 19 subjects were women. The 13 control subjects were all men.

Public Assistance. Seventeen of the unwanted children (14.2 percent) had received some form of public assistance between the ages of 16 and 21, and 3 of the control subjects (2.5 percent). The difference is significant ($0.005 > p > 0.001$).

Only one subject, a boy in the control series, received a disablement pension from the government; he was an idiot and permanently institutionalized.

Educational Subnormality. Under this heading we included all the uneducable subjects, the ones taught in special schools for the mentally retarded, those whose last year at school was spent in a special class. In the last group we also included a few subjects whose educational subnormality was well documented, but who were taught in ordinary classes because there was no form of special training available for them.

The large cities have a graduated series of special classes in the ordinary schools called remedial reading classes, observation classes, extra classes and health classes, but we paid no attention to the kind of special class the subject pupils attended, mostly because where they lived determined what kind of class they could choose from.

According to these criteria, 13 of the unwanted children (10.8 percent) were educationally subnormal, as against 6 of the control subjects (5.0 percent). This difference is not significant ($p = 0.10$).

There was one case of well documented mental retardation both in the original and in the control series.

Theoretical Studies Beyond the Obligatory. On drawing a line between the subjects who had done more advanced theoretical study than that required by the school law, and those who had not, we found that only 17 (14.2 percent) of the unwanted had had some form of higher education, as against 40 (33.3 percent) of the control subjects. The difference is highly significant ($p < 0.001$).

Eight unwanted and 12 control children had taken university entrance examinations. Five unwanted children and 11 control children had studied at a university. Neither of these differences is significant.

As mentioned (table 2), more of the control than original subjects came from social group II and the reverse was true for social group III. As a child's education depends a great deal on the social standing of its parents, we also compared the schooling in the two series after excluding the subjects left over when the two kinds of subjects were paired according to social group. This left 77 subjects in each series. Ten of these 77 (13.0 percent) unwanted children had had some form of higher education, against 21 of the 77 control children (27.3 percent). The difference is probably significant ($p < 0.05$).

One can also study the effect of social standing on the education by taking one social group at a time; for this we had to combine groups I and II, as there were too few cases in group I. Five of the 95 unwanted children (5.3 percent) coming from group III had had higher education, against 17 of the 84 control subjects (20.2 percent) coming from the same social group. The difference is significant (p <0.01). The figures for group I + II were 11 out of 25 (44.0 percent) against 28 out of 36 (77.8 percent). Here the difference is probably significant (p <0.05).

Continuing with these calculations, chi square amounts to 7.93 for social group III and to 5.89 for I and II combined. The sum, 13.82, with 2 degrees of freedom gives a p of <0.001, showing a highly significant difference for the three social groups combined.

Thus it was not differences in proportion of different social groups that caused the difference in schooling between the unwanted and control children.

Military Service. Ten of the 66 males in the original series (15.2 percent) were judged unfit for military service, either at the time of enrollment or after they had started, as opposed to 4 (6.7 percent) of the control subjects. This is not a significant difference (0.20 >p> 0.10). According to our information, 4 of the 10 first males were exempted for mental reasons; our information in this respect may not be complete, however. Two of the control subjects were exempted on these grounds.

When a Swedish recruit enrolls, he is classified into one of four groups according to his fitness for military service, from group 1 for a completely satisfactory condition down to group 4 who are assigned to fatigue duty. Apart from exemption from service, our two series were distributed very much alike by fitness for military service.

Marital Status and Parenthood. As we only followed our subjects up to the age of 21, we cannot say much about how they compare with regard to marriage and parenthood. Some differences did emerge, however.

Twenty of the unwanted children (17 women, 3 men) married before the age of 21, and 14 of the control subjects (9 women, 5 men). The difference is not significant here, either for the sexes combined or for one of them.

Two of the female subjects from the original series had also divorced before the age of 21; none of the control women had done so, and no man from either series.

We restricted our analysis of parenthood to the women, as there was no hope of getting reliable figures for the men in this respect. Fourteen out of 54 women from the original series had had 19 children before they were 21, 4 out of wedlock, and 7 of the 54 female control subjects had had 9 children, 3 out of wedlock.

It is impossible to draw any conclusions from these figures. It will be noted, however, that the control series (which had more education on the whole) contained fewer cases of early marriage and of young mothers. This tallies with the observation that the age of marriage and parenthood rises with the degree of education.

Freedom from Defect in All Respects Studied. Sometimes the same subject will occur in more than one of the groups studied here. Thus a subject registered with the authorities for abuse of alcohol will often be found in the files of the centers for child psychiatry as well; a man who has been in a mental hospital will sometimes be exempted from military service; an uneducable subject will be registered as receiving public assistance, as being educated in a special class, and so on. It is interesting, therefore, to compare the two series for the number of subjects showing no defect in any of the respects studied, i.e., registration for antisocial behavior in the books of the child welfare boards or penal register; official registration for drunken misconduct; education in a special class or school, or uneducability; public assistance or government pension; visits to psychiatric inpatient or outpatient departments during childhood or adulthood. Fifty-eight (48.3 percent) of the unwanted children showed none of these defects against 82 (68.3 percent) of the control subjects. The difference is significant ($0.005 > p > 0.001$).

Taking social group III separately from I and II combined showed the following: Forty of the 95 unwanted children (42.1 percent) coming from group III showed no defect, against 54 of the 84 control subjects (64.3 percent) from the same group. The difference is significant ($0.005 > p > 0.001$). The corresponding figures for group I and II combined were 19 out of 25 (76.0 percent) against 28 out of 36 (77.8 percent). Here the difference is not significant.

The same analysis of the 77 pairs concordant for social group gave 34 unwanted cases (44.2 percent) showing no defect, against 54 control (70.1 percent). The difference is significant ($0.005 > p > 0.001$).

Similar analysis of the 55 pairs living in Göteborg the whole time gave 20 (36.4 percent) showing no defect against 38 (69.1 percent). The difference is highly significant ($p < 0.001$).

As children from broken homes are more apt than others to be antisocial and mentally disturbed, we compared the two series for the number of cases showing none of the aforementioned defects among the subjects who had lived with both their real parents until they were 15. Thirty-three out of the 60 such subjects from the original series (55.0 percent) showed none of these defects, and 68 out of the 98 control subjects of this category (69.4 percent). The difference is not significant ($0.10 > p > 0.05$).

Discussion

Table 4 gives a survey of the ways in which the children born after their mother had been refused a legal abortion differed from the control series of same-aged subjects chosen at random. As seen there, the unwanted children were worse off in every respect, the only exception being due to the one case of a government pension which came from the control series. The differences were often significant, and when they were not, they pointed in the same direction (except for the case just mentioned)—to a worse lot for the unwanted children.

When one looks for a reason for the differences, one is struck mostly by the greater frequency of factors tending to disrupt the stability of the home in the case of the unwanted children, such as birth out of wedlock, and death or divorce of their parents while they were still young. In other words, not as many unwanted children were brought up by both their real parents as were control subjects. Probably as a corollary of this, more of them were brought up by foster parents or in children's homes. But the latter may also have been a con-

Table 4. Survey of important differences between the unwanted and control children

	Unwanted children			Control children			Level of sign. of differ.
	No. in resp. series	Feature present No.	%	No. in resp. series	Feature present No.	%	
Psychiatric consultation and hospitalization	120	34	28.3	120	18	15.0	*
Registration for delinquency at children's aid bureaus	120	22	18.3	120	10	8.3	*
Registration for crime in Penal Register	120	10	8.3	120	3	2.5	—
Registration for drunken misconduct	120	19	15.8	120	13	10.8	—
Public assistance between ages of 16 and 21	120	17	14.2	120	3	2.5	**
Subnormal educability or uneducability	120	13	10.8	120	6	5.0	—
Theoretical studies beyond the obligatory:							
Whole series	120	17	14.2	120	40	33.3	***
Subjects in pairs congruent for social group	77	10	13.0	77	21	27.3	*
Subjects from social group III	95	5	5.3	84	17	20.2	**
Subjects from social groups I + II	25	11	44.0	36	28	77.8	*
Exemption from military service	66	10	15.2	66	4	6.7	—
Freedom from inferiority in above respects:							
Whole series	120	58	48.3	120	82	68.3	**
Social group III	95	40	42.1	84	54	64.3	**
Social groups I + II	25	19	76.0	36	28	77.8	—
Subjects in pairs congruent for social group	77	34	44.2	77	54	70.1	**
Subjects living all their life in Göteborg	55	20	36.4	55	38	69.1	***
Subjects brought up by both their real parents	60	33	55.0	98	68	69.4	—

sequence of the greater number of complaints to the children's welfare boards about the way in which they were being treated at home.

The difference that turned up most consistently in various forms of analysis was the difference in amount of education. Whatever categories of subjects were studied—different social ranks or different subgroups of the same social rank—the unwanted children got a significantly smaller amount of education than the control subjects.

The reason the unwanted children had had so much contact with psychiatrists was probably not—as we showed—that their mothers found it easier to consult a psychiatrist about their child because they had once before consulted a psychiatrist about themselves. It was probably because these mothers were more vulnerable mentally than the others, and passed on this failing to their children, either through genes or through the effect it had on the home environment, or both.

The investigation has shown that children born after their mothers have been refused permission for legal abortion are born into a worse situation than other children. From this one may assume that the children who are not born because their mothers get authorization for abortion would have had to face still greater disadvantages, socially and mentally. Thus, the very fact that a woman seeks an authorized abortion, no matter how trivial her grounds may appear to some, means that the expected child will run a larger risk than its peers of an inferior standing in life. In our opinion, the present investigation shows that the provisions for therapeutic abortion in the law should not only aim to prevent the private tragedy; they should also aim to improve mental hygiene in a wider sense. Thus the legislation should also consider the social handicaps awaiting the unwanted child, not only, as it does now, the genetic risk in the narrow sense of the terms.

Summary

The authors examined 120 children born after their mothers had applied for therapeutic abortion on psychiatric grounds and been refused, comparing them with an appropriate control series of the same size. All the subjects studied lived and were followed up until the age of 21. Data were assembled from civil and ecclesiastical registry offices, social agencies, school authorities, military authorities and all the psychiatric inpatient and outpatient departments everywhere the subjects had lived. It was ascertained how many of each series had been registered for mental ill-health, antisocial and criminal actions, drunken misconduct, and different forms of public assistance; for the men it was ascertained how they had got on during their military service; likewise the marital status, number of children, and school ability and educational level was [sic] determined.

A study of the social features revealed that many more of the unwanted than control children had not had the advantage of a secure family life during childhood. They were also registered more often in psychiatric services, and a few more of them than control subjects received psychiatric care. They were more often registered for antisocial and criminal behavior, and slightly more often for drunken misconduct, and they got public assistance more often than the control subjects. A few more of them were educationally subnormal and far fewer had pursued theoretical studies over and above what is obligatory. They were more often exempted from military service. More of the females married early and had children early than in the control series. The differences between the two series in these respects were often statistically significant, and when they were not significant they always pointed in the same direction—to the unwanted children being born into a worse situation than the control children. Table 4 gives figures for most of the features just mentioned.

The authors conclude that the very fact a woman applies for legal abortion means that the prospective child runs a risk of having to surmount greater social and mental handicaps than its peers, even when the grounds for the application are so slight that it is refused. In their opinion, the legislation of therapeutic termination of pregnancy should also consider the social risks to which the expected child will be exposed.

APPENDIX D

Reading List

The following titles are only a small part of the literature on abortion, but they contain references to most of the important works.

Callahan, Daniel. *Abortion: Law, Choice and Morality.* New York: Macmillan, 1970. This is the most scholarly study in print, rich in documentation. By a liberal Catholic.

Cooke, Robert E. *et al.*, eds. *The Terrible Choice.* New

York: Bantam Books, 1968. Includes scenarios designed to create anxiety in women who are contemplating elective abortion. Also included are some of the photographs of embryos used by Right-to-Life lecturers, though they are here presented only in black and white.

Hardin, Garrett. *Stalking the Wild Taboo*. Los Altos, Calif.: William Kaufmann, 1973. Most of the documentation of statements made in the present book can be found in the first ten chapters of this collection of essays.

Hindell, Keith, and Madeleine Simms. *Abortion Law Reformed*. London: Peter Owen, 1971. A thorough history of the successful campaign to liberalize the abortion laws in Great Britain.

Lader, Lawrence. *Abortion*. Indianapolis: Bobbs-Merrill, 1966; Boston: Beacon Press, 1967. This is the most widely known proabortion treatise written by one who has been a vigorous activist in the field for many years.

———. *Abortion II: Making the Revolution*. Boston: Beacon Press, 1973. Completes Lader's history of the abortion fight from 1966 to the Supreme Court decision in 1973. Warns of impending "Right-to-Life" challenge.

Noonan, John T., Jr. *Contraception*. Cambridge, Mass.: Harvard University Press, 1965. Only a small part of this voluminous work is devoted to abortion, but it is worth looking at to see how an orthodox and legalistic Catholic approaches the issue.

Osofsky, Howard J. and Joy D., eds. *The Abortion Experience*. New York: Harper and Row, 1973. A wide-ranging account of medical, psychological, and social aspects of abortion in the United States.

Reiterman, Carl, ed. *Abortion and the Unwanted Child.* New York: Springer, 1971. A series of papers emphasizing the harm done to children by a system which produces unwanted children.

Tietze, Christopher, and Deborah A. Dawson. *Induced Abortion: A Factbook.* New York: The Population Council, 1973. For statistics on abortion all over the world this is the absolute bible. Number, frequency, distribution by maternal and fetal age, mortality, morbidity, and many other variables are thoroughly documented herein.

APPENDIX E

Educational and Activist Organizations

Those who feel a call to help in putting an end to mandatory motherhood should consider supporting these three societies.

ASA. Association for the Study of Abortion
120 West 57th Street
New York, N.Y. 10019

This organization confines its efforts to education (no political action). It keeps its members informed about legislative developments, and it reprints and distributes significant articles and legal decisions.

The following two organizations are politically active in the area of abortion.

NOW. National Organization of Women
   1957 East 73rd Street
   Chicago, Ill. 60649

NARAL. National Abortion Rights Action League
   250 West 57th Street
   New York, N.Y. 10019